Progressivism

A Primer on the Idea Destroying America

By James Ostrowski

Cazenovia Books

Buffalo, New York (U. S. A.)

LibertyMovement.org

Published by Cazenovia Books, Buffalo, New York

Printed in the United States of America

ISBN 978-09749253-87

First Edition

In Honor of

William J. and Mary V. Ostrowski

When the wine stirred in their heart their bosoms dilated.
They rose to suppose themselves kings over all things created –
To decree a new earth at a birth without labour or sorrow –
To declare: "We prepare it to-day and inherit to-morrow."
They chose themselves prophets and priests of minute understanding,
Men swift to see done, and outrun, their extremest commanding –
Of the tribe which describe with a jibe the perversions of Justice –
Panders avowed to the crowd whatsoever its lust is.

---City of Brass, Rudyard Kipling

Contents

Acknowledgements   i

Foreword   iii

Introduction   1

1.   What is Progressivism?   21
2.   We Are All Progressives Now   37
3.   The Origins of Progressivism   41
4.   The Failure of Progressivism   51
5.   Progressivism's Archenemy—
    True Liberalism   91
6.   Progressivism's Vanquished Foe—
    Conservatism   123
7.   War is the Health of the Progressive State   137
8.   Progressivism as Utopianism   147
9.   A Rogue's Gallery of Progressives   151
10.   How to Bury Progressivism and
    Restore American Liberty   167

Conclusion   195

Bibliography   203

Index   207

About the Author   214

Acknowledgements

This book was conceived and chapters outlined on Sunday, April 15, 2012, the holiest day on the progressive calendar. I also had in mind the effective end of the second Ron Paul campaign and was cognizant of the need to continue the Revolution after the campaign ended.

Due to the day job, it was a struggle to finish the first draft by July 15, 2014 and prepare the book for publication.

I want to thank all the people, especially my family and friends who, without any hope of personal reward, aided in my many political endeavors over the years. I can't possibly name them all but I remember each of you and I will never forget your kindnesses. Please know that I have never given up the fight regardless of temporary setbacks. This book, which your efforts helped produce, is proof of that.

My intellectual debts are also too numerous to mention. Three stand out. My late father, William J. Ostrowski, a brilliant lawyer and passionate civil libertarian, taught me how to think critically and logically. If I have accomplished anything as a lawyer, it is because I am the only graduate of the W. J. O. School of Law.

Second, Thomas Jefferson. He has many critics and was much better out of office than in it, but no one can deny that he stated the basic doctrine of liberty earlier and better and with greater impact than almost anyone else.

Finally, Murray Rothbard, whom I had the honor of knowing. I can honestly say that I was his student, having attended his seminar on the history of economic thought in the 1980's in Manhattan. His influence is felt throughout the book which is no surprise since the first time I heard him speak in 1980, the subject was the Progressives and World War I.

In researching this book, I have relied heavily on a group of libertarian scholars affiliated with the Mises Institute: Ralph Raico, Tom Dilorenzo, Tom Woods, Guido Hülsmann, Hans-Hermann Hoppe and Robert Higgs. I also greatly benefitted from the works of two other prolific libertarian scholars, Jim Powell and George Smith.

Finally, a special thanks to the man who has been the unofficial leader of the Liberty Movement since Murray Rothbard died in 1995— Lew Rockwell. I have benefitted from his voluminous and lucid writings, his website, LewRockwell.com, which I read daily and write for occasionally, and from the vast online resources of the Mises Institute which I used innumerable times in the preparation of this book. Please support the Mises Institute and LewRockwell.com.

****

Please note that I started a website, LibertyMovement.org, to carry out the strategic and tactical ideas proposed in the book.

James Ostrowski
Buffalo, New York
October 2014

Foreword

This book is the culmination of forty-five years of involvement in politics. My father became a judge when I was four years old. The first campaign I actually worked on was his re-election campaign for Buffalo City Court in 1970 when I was 12 years old. Even before that, I would overhear Mom on the phone talking about the latest political news. It was Mom, not Dad, who unwittingly taught me my first lessons about politics: it was a dirty rotten business filled with scoundrels. Nothing I was to learn from firsthand experience in politics and later anti-politics ever contradicted Mom's first lesson.

From about 1975 through 1979, I worked furiously inside the Democratic Party trying to reform politics and defeat the machine.[1] In 1978, at age 20, I ran a competitive race for New York State Assembly in the Democratic Party, forcing the party to import party hacks from all over the state to support the machine candidate. An Assemblyman *from the Bronx* knocked on my next-door neighbor Carl's door. Imagine the chutzpah! Carl told him to go peddle his papers somewhere else.

I joined the Liberty Movement in 1979 having discovered Murray Rothbard via Ayn Rand and Robert Nozick who cited Murray and tried to refute him in *Anarchy, State and Utopia*, a book assigned in Paul Kurtz's course in political thought at the University of Buffalo.

Thus, this book is the product of 36 years of intense involvement in the Movement in a variety of different capacities. Since the Liberty Movement is fairly new, dating from about 1968, I have been involved in it for the vast majority of its existence. And, because the movement

---

[1] Those years are discussed in *Political Class Dismissed* (2004).

was very small when I got involved, I very quickly got to know many of the key figures including Rothbard. There has never been a time in the Movement when I did not consider myself a Rothbardian. I did not meet Ron Paul until much later (1988) but served as his election law attorney in New York State in 2008 and was heavily involved in both of his presidential campaigns. I have worked with many of the key Movement organizations over the years including the Mises Institute, the Cato Institute and the Libertarian Party.

My experience in electoral politics is quite diverse. Over the years, I have been active in the Democratic, Republican and Libertarian parties. I have been involved in two major candidacies run on independent lines including a race for Congress that got national publicity. I was heavily involved in the early days of the Tea Party Movement but eventually left the movement after it was co-opted by the GOP and thereby self-destructed. I spent my first five years out of law school trying to end the drug war and wrote a major study for the Cato Institute on the subject. I have practiced election law for many years, largely because there were few lawyers around who would fight the machine's efforts to remove candidates from the ballot. I have also been a paid consultant in recent years and have worked for a variety of candidates.

I say all this not to pat myself on the back but to provide the reader with a factual basis to judge my credibility in making what are admittedly sweeping and controversial assertions about the Movement and about the need to move away from politics—elections and lobbying—and toward direct citizen action as our primary strategy. I did not come by the approach of direct action by pure cogitation and philosophizing as much as I was driven to the conclusion that direct action is our only real hope because all else had failed and failed repeatedly and dramatically! Those who wish the Liberty Movement to fail should continue to do what we have been doing and ignore the strategic and tactical proposals in this book.

In that spirit, this book follows logically from my prior three books and thus completes a quadrilogy. My first book, *Political Class Dismissed (2004)*, explained the basics of applied libertarianism and why the natural tendency of government is to grow and why politics is a rigged game. My second book, *Government Schools Are Bad for Your Kids*

Foreword

(2009), took direct aim at the very foundation of big government in America by means of direct action and the only "school choice" worthy of the name: the fatal choice to send or *not send* your precious offspring to a government youth detention and propaganda center. My third book, *Direct Citizen Action (2010)*, expanded the concept of direct action and laid out a detailed set of direct action strategies to achieve liberty.

Yet, these books *did not* achieve the desired results. Their failure forced me to dig far deeper into the foundations of an American statism that was so resilient as to brush off not only my own modest efforts to put a dent into it, but also casually respond to the efforts of the best libertarian minds to "smash the state" by getting even larger and more powerful more quickly.

The result of that labor is this book. The Liberty Movement will continue to fail until it manages to eradicate the mindset that is destroying America.

Granted, I have been deeply ensconced in the *Liberty Movement* for decades but what qualifies me to write about the progressive mindset? That's an easy one. I have lived in the progressive capital of the country, New York State, for my entire life (counting four years sleeping in New Jersey). I lived in New York City for four years. I went to a progressive university and a progressive law school. I was a progressive of sorts in my youth albeit with libertarian leanings and I worked on Ramsey Clark's 1974 Senate campaign.

Unlike some in the movement, I have spent most of my life talking to progressives not fellow travelers. I have been debating with progressives since 1979. Many of my friends and relatives are progressives. I have probably had thousands of political discussions with progressives which constitute the "lab work" for this book. I know whereof I speak.

Introduction

America is dying from an idea she only dimly understands, so-called "progressivism." Progressivism is an ideology with no basis in fact or logic. Its original proponents believed it to be a scientific approach to politics.[2] That is "nonsense on stilts," to quote back at them a sneer about natural law by the proto-progressive Jeremy Bentham. Progressivism was not subjected to any sort of scientific testing before it became the ruling ideology in America around 1900. Nor have its many policy revolutions ever been tested scientifically. Rather, a bad idea was propagated, spread and was installed as the dominant guide to policy and dramatically changed the nature of America for the worse. America will continue its downward spiral until this false and destructive ideology is fully understood and rejected.

Progressivism may be initially defined as the strong presumption that democratic government intervention (force) will produce a better result than voluntary society. Hence the root of the word "progress". However, the "progress" element of progressivism is aspirational, not factual. The term begs the question by assuming as true that which has not been proved: that progressive ideas will lead to progress. In fact, while progressives portray themselves as scientific, pragmatic, result-oriented and fact-based, there is little evidence, scientific or otherwise, that progressive programs have improved society. See, Chapter 4.

Progressivism has been the dominant political force since at least 1912 when all three major candidates for President were progressives.

---

[2] See, Andrew Feffer, *The Chicago Pragmatists and American Progressivism*, Cornell University Press, 1993, pp. 5-6.; M. Rothbard, "Origin of the Welfare State in America," *Journal of Libertarian Studies*, 12:2 (Fall 1996), 193, 222.

Introduction

Major elements of the progressive program were installed shortly thereafter. The income tax amendment took effect in 1913. The Federal Reserve was also created in 1913. These two acts combined had the impact of allowing the federal government direct access to the nation's income and wealth either by taxation or inflation of the money supply. These complementary means of wealth acquisition would allow the federal government to pay for the numerous progressive programs rolled out in the ensuing 100 years and presently.

Progressive Era programs were built on the foundation laid by the Civil War which was the federal government's first great leap forward in establishing dominance over the states and the people. The New Deal added several new programs including Social Security, the minimum wage, agricultural subsidies and public housing and granted unions the power to force businesses to bargain with them. The Great Society began to socialize medicine with Medicare and Medicaid and vastly expanded the welfare state. Throughout the entire period, coercive regulation of business and everyday life by federal, state and local government steadily increased.

"Regulation" in this context is one of those words whose mellifluent sound belies its ugly reality. Regulations ban peaceful voluntary behavior that is neither criminal, tortious nor violative of any contract. A regulation is a tax on non-monetary wealth: time, energy, and property. The sum total of all regulations destroys untold amounts of wealth and does so in such a stealthy manner that only the most discerning economists and policy analysts even notice.

One way to better understand the impact of regulations is what I call the *forced purchase theory of the state*. Almost everything the progressive state does can be conceived as a *forced purchase*. The state, through taxation and regulation, *makes us poorer* by forcing us directly or indirectly to buy crap we don't want, don't need and can't afford. Perhaps it is anomalous to characterize as a purchase a transaction done at the point of the state's gun, however, that is what the state and its proponents think they are doing. They don't think they are stealing from us. They think they are making us do something that is good for us and they purport to take our money via taxes and provide some product or service they think we need. Or, in the case of regulations, they think they are making us buy a better product or service than what we would buy if left to our own devices. Thus, I think it is wise to deal with these forced purchases in a straightforward manner and explain why they are actually bad for us and make us poorer.

I also believe there are rhetorical advantages to this approach. In spite of the growth of the Liberty Movement in recent years, libertarians have been unsuccessful in explaining their philosophy and gaining new converts beyond about ten percent of the population. We have certainly failed to roll back the State and in fact, as our movement grows, so does the State and even faster! For example, very few members of the American public, 80% of whom are in some sense broke or living week to week, blame the government for their plight. They are more likely to blame the greed of large corporations. I believe by explaining why a massive amount of forced purchases makes us poorer, we can make the public better understand the truly catastrophic and deleterious economic impact of the State on their daily lives. No other approach has worked so far in the 45-year life of the Liberty Movement.

Where do we stand with progressivism at this time? Virtually every aspect of our lives is to some extent or entirely controlled or regulated by the state. At birth, our children are forced into the Social Security system and subjected to a variety of mandatory tests and vaccines. They start out life owing about $55,000, representing their per capita share of the federal debt imposed on them to pay for the campaign promises of dead politicians.[3] Our children are kidnapped from their homes and placed into daytime juvenile detention and propaganda centers (government schools) at age six.

Our sons are forced to register for the draft and, thanks to the progressives, can be drafted at any time for any reason and sent overseas to die in a foreign war for ill-defined purposes. They are forced to engage in *unpaid* child labor in government schools, but they cannot do *paid* work of their own choosing, pushing many of them into black market activity or illegal forms of work many of which are extremely dangerous or sordid. Progressives claim to have abolished child labor, but juvenile prisons are crammed with kids who were *working* in the underground economy.

The health care industry is almost entirely under the control of government via licensing, regulation and subsidies. Over half of all

---

[3] *Source*: brillig.com/debt_clock

medical expenses are paid for by government, which leads to government control over how such funds are spent.[4] For the first time ever, every American is now required to purchase or maintain health insurance.

On average, government takes as much as half of every dollar Americans earn.[5]

Government controls the money supply and can expand it at will merely by typing numbers onto a computer screen—easier than growing money on trees. Government can and does regulate or ban outright any market-based forms of money.

Virtually every aspect of business is controlled by the state. One cannot enter a large number of professions without a license or a permit. For several years, the author has wanted to start a company to sell information to consumers that is not available in any other form. I have, however, been unable to do so as state and federal laws make it a *crime* to sell such information. Even if a license or permit is not required, there are so many regulations and taxes imposed on any small company with employees that it is quite difficult for the average person without large sums of money to start a business.

Before the Progressive Era, one could travel around the world freely with few legal obstructions. Today, that right is eroding. One needs the permission of the state to travel. Rumor has it that Americans may soon need permission just to leave the country. The state may strip-search you and your family on re-entry to the "freest country on earth" and "sweet land of liberty." Government now claims the right to search you without probable cause at airports, bus stations and trains stations.

Formerly, if you followed the rules of the road, you could drive around the government roads unmolested. No longer. Now, you are watched and recorded everywhere. Your behavior *inside the car* is now strictly regulated with, for example, Luddite bans on cell phone use while driving. Thankfully, there is widespread resistance to this idiotic

---

[4] C. Conover, "Takeover: Government On Track To Make Up 66% of Healthcare Spending," *Forbes.com*, Aug. 7, 2012.

[5] P. Tyrrell, "Government Will Take Almost Half Your Paycheck in 2013," *blog.heritage.org*, Aug. 13, 2012.

law, demonstrating that there remains a kernel of American gumption among the population. However, as long as the silly cliché, "driving is a privilege, not a right," is taken as Gospel truth by government judges, there will be no end to annoying new laws restricting our freedom to travel in peace, quiet and privacy.

If you travel abroad, *it is a liability to be an American.* The Progressive State of America (PSA) has been intervening into the internal affairs of other countries since the time of the first war progressives helped to instigate: the Spanish-American War in 1898. Over time, resentment has developed against Americans in many countries. There is also the real risk, albeit small, of being murdered by a terrorist retaliating against this or that intervention into his own country by Uncle Sam. "[T]he majority of suicide terrorism around the world since 1980 has had a common cause: military occupation."[6] The government itself admits this:

> "The Department of State remains concerned about the continued threat of terrorist attacks, demonstrations, and other violent actions against U.S. citizens and interests overseas. Current information suggests that al-Qa'ida, its affiliated organizations, and other terrorist groups continue to plan terrorist attacks against U.S. interests in multiple regions, including Europe, Asia, Africa, and the Middle East. These attacks may employ a wide variety of tactics including suicide operations, assassinations, kidnappings, hijackings, and bombings."[7]

The progressive approach of better living through the brandishing of government guns has drawn the Progressive State of America into an endless series of destructive and expensive foreign wars, large, medium and small, covert and all too well-known. Bob Dole was right to call them "Democrat wars." He might as well have called them "progressive wars." As discussed in detail in Chapter 7, *progressives love*

---

[6] L. Rozen, "Researcher: Suicide terrorism linked to military occupation," *Politico.com*, Oct. 11, 2010.
[7] Worldwide Caution, September 25, 2013.

war. The PSA has been involved in 46 wars since and including World War I.[8] The PSA has "164,227 of its active-duty personnel serving outside the United States and its territories and an additional 118,966 deployed in various contingency operations. PSA troops are spread across the globe: over 66,000 are stationed in Europe; over 51,000 in East Asia and the Pacific region; over 4,500 in North Africa, the Near East, and South Asia . . ."[9]

Thus, the progressive program has been executed to a very large extent. Furthermore, as discussed in Chapter 1, progressivism has no limiting principle or stopping point. The process by which the progressive mindset causes increases in the size, scope and power of government never ceases. Robert Wenzel, a leading Liberty Movement blogger, posted a list of things that were *legal* in 1975 but are *illegal* now:

> "In 1975:
>
> 1. You could buy an airline ticket and fly without ever showing an ID.
> 2. You could buy cough syrup without showing an ID.
> 3. You could buy and sell gold coins without showing an ID.
> 4. You could buy a gun without showing an ID.
> 5. You could pull as much cash out of your bank account without the bank filing a report with the government.
> 6. You could get a job without having to prove you were an American.
> 7. You could buy cigarettes without showing an ID.
> 8. You could have a phone conversation without the government knowing who you called and who called you.

---

[8] en.wikipedia.org/wiki/List_of_wars_involving_the_United_States.
[9] Source: en.wikipedia.org/wiki/United_States_military_deployments

9. You could open a stock brokerage account without having to explain where the money came from.
10. You could open a Swiss bank account with ease. All Swiss banks were willing and happy to open accounts for Americans.

There are thousands of other examples."[10]

Government has been growing steadily and rapidly since the dawn of the Progressive Era; is growing now and will continue to grow unless that mindset is replaced or eliminated or until the state collapses under its own weight or is overthrown by revolution or civil war. Short of one of those contingencies, *under progressivism, the state will grow until it controls everything and absolutely. That is, it will grow into a totalitarian state.*

Having already executed a substantial portion of its program, we must ask, how is progressive America doing in 2014?

THE ECONOMY

The American economy is a mess and average Americans struggle to pay their bills each week while working longer hours than they did in 1973 and usually having both spouses working outside the home.

A record number of adults 25-34 are living with their parents, 13 percent, up from 10 percent in the early 2000s.[11]

About 16 percent of Americans bounce checks each year, costing them about $32 billion dollars annually,[12] money they apparently cannot afford. (At the same time, banks get loans of cheap money from the progressive's Federal Reserve.) Obviously, the problem is not

---

[10] "Liberty Slipping: 10 Things You Could Do in 1975 That You Can't Do Now," *EconomicPolicyJournal.com*, July 2, 2013.
[11] N. Shah, "More Young Adults Live With Parents," *WSJ.com*, Aug. 27, 2013.
[12] E. Melendez, "U.S. Overdraft Fees Jump To $32 Billion As New Rules Prove Ineffective (*HuffingonPost.com*, March 29, 2013.).

simply being disorganized but frequently having a low or zero balance in their accounts.

Almost 11 million Americans are now receiving disability benefits, a record.[13] The number of Americans on disability has increased for 201 straight months. This is in spite of the fact that rapid advances in technology should have resulted in *fewer* people unable to work.

Americans owe over one trillion dollars in student loans.[14] Student loan debt has increased rapidly in recent years.

Americans owe $16 billion in child support payments and another $41 billion in hospital bills.[15]

About 35 percent of Americans are over 180 days late on paying bills.[16]

The Federal debt is over $17 trillion.[17] Your share is about $55,000. The current annual deficit is $680 billion and the annual interest on the debt is over $200 billion. It's not clear how this debt can be paid off without hyperinflation which could lead to a collapse of the economy.

According to a 2012 study by Credit Suisse Bank, the median wealth of Americans is just $38,786. Much of that small sum is likely to be tied up in the home they live in, if they are lucky enough to own a home and have equity in it. That means the only way they could spend any of their net worth is by selling or mortgaging their house! These folks face a grim economic future as they grow older.

According to a survey by Bankrate:

> "More than three-fourths of Americans don't have enough money saved to pay their bills for six months. . . Half of the survey respondents said they had less than three months' worth of expenses saved up . . . and

[13] *CNSNews.com* (Dec. 31, 2013).

[14] S. Frizzell, "Student Loans Are Ruining Your Life. Now They're Ruining the Economy, Too," *Time*, Feb. 6, 2014.

[15] B. Japsen, "Unpaid Hospital Bills Rise To $41 Billion Annually," *Forbes.com*, Jan. 7, 2013.

[16] H. Malcom, "A third of Americans delinquent on debt," *USA Today*, July 29, 2014.

[17] En.wikipedia.org/wiki/National_debt_of_the_United_States

more than one-quarter . . . have no reserves to draw on in case of emergency."[18]

The average American suffers from permanent inflation created by one of the twin pillars of progressivism, the Federal Reserve. Inflation is bad for many reasons, most importantly, because it causes malinvestment and the boom and bust cycle which destroys the dreams and hopes of millions every few years or so. However, inflation also redistributes wealth on a daily basis from the working class—private sector workers and business owners—to the political class, those who make their livings substantially or entirely through government. Technically, those who receive newly-created money first—government employees, pensioners, welfare and "entitlement" recipients, government contractors and banks—get to spend the new money at currently existing prices. This spending bids up prices and raises the cost of living for the rest of us.[19] As Guido Hülsmann argues, inflation tends to redistribute wealth from the average person to the wealthy and thus hinders upward social mobility.[20]

When wages are measured in terms of hard assets such as gold or gasoline, we see in clear terms what most of us already feel: we are getting poorer! "In terms of gold, wages have fallen by about 87 percent" since 1965.[21]

In recent years, there have been record numbers of people unemployed, collecting unemployment benefits and staying on unemployment longer. Scamming unemployment is a tradition now firmly ensconced in American culture. Seasonal and temporary workers routinely file for unemployment instead of working or

---

[18] J. Berman, "75 Percent Of Americans Don't Have Enough Savings To Cover Their Bills For Six Months: Survey," *Huffington Post,* June 24, 2013.

[19] Murray N. Rothbard, *The Mystery of Banking,* 2nd ed. 2008, pp. 53-54. Auburn: Ludwig von Mises Institute.

[20] "How Inflation Helps Keep the Rich Up and the Poor Down," *Mises Audio Daily,* June 4, 2014.

[21] K. Weiner, "Measured In Gold, The Story Of American Wages Is An Ugly One," *Forbes.com,* Oct. 9, 2013.

seriously seeking employment. There is an amazing coincidence in many cases wherein the individual manages to get a job the week his or her unemployment benefits run out. All this is done openly with a complete absence of the shame that used to accompany idleness.

Unemployment insurance is one of the more blatantly irrational progressive programs. The notion that it is in the interest of society to systematically pay people not to work is obviously stupid. It also illustrates a point discussed throughout the book: progressives have no theory of costs. Progressive programs make sense only if you assume they have zero cost, an obvious absurdity. Among the several problems with unemployment insurance is the fact that the program raises the costs of hiring new workers, thus tending to *increase unemployment* particularly among younger and lesser-skilled workers who lack a track record of keeping jobs for long periods of time.

Overall, unemployment insurance erodes the work ethic, increases dependency on government, costs the economy billions of dollars and makes it more difficult for firms to hire new workers. Unemployment insurance amounts to *a tax on ambition* as those who refuse to remain idle end up subsidizing those who relish it.

According to the Heritage Foundation, "the number of people receiving benefits from the federal government in the United States has grown from under 94 million people in 2000 to more than 128 million people in 2011. That means that 41.3 percent of the U.S. population is now on a federal government program."[22]

As the American Dream has become increasingly remote from the poor and working class, Americans have creatively sought out substitutes for attaining the brass ring. Spending on lottery tickets is at an all-time high. Americans spent over $65 billion on lottery tickets in 2012.[23] Shoplifting has become a major crime with as many as 550,000 incidents a day and costing $13 billion annually.[24] Television ads and billboards constantly remind us that we could be rich if we were

---

[22] P. Tyrrell and W. Beach, "U.S. Government Increases National Debt—and Keeps 128 Million People on Government Programs," Jan. 8, 2013.

[23] money.cnn.com/2012/11/27/news/economy/powerball-lottery-sales/index.html

[24] Source: National Association of Shoplifting Prevention.

"injured" and want to sue. In many neighborhoods, the odds of getting rich in court seem greater than the odds of getting rich by starting a business.

Many Americans in recent years have run up huge credit card debts in order to maintain their standard of living during a period of economic decline. Total credit card debt is $854.2 billion with an average of $7,000 per capita.[25] One study found that 64% of Americans could not come up with $1000 cash if an emergency arose.[26]

When the right to liberty was, by and large, respected in America, the culture promoted a strong work ethic and a willingness to take risks to start exciting new businesses and invent new products. As the doors of liberty and economic opportunity have closed, the old-fashioned *work ethic* has increasingly been replaced by a *scam ethic*, various gimmicks, chicanery and manipulations, some legal, some illegal, some borderline, to maintain one's standard of living in a declining economy. In an older America, families were somehow able to buy Christmas presents for their children without disrupting Thanksgiving with the insanity of Black Friday.

HEALTH

Obesity plagues about one-third of adults and 20 percent of children over age five.[27] Bigger government makes you fatter, apparently. Obesity has skyrocketed in recent years as progressive government has grown. Is there a causal connection? *Yes*. Obesity is largely a function of low levels of human capital. Human capital is the sum total of all the skills, knowledge and character traits that successful living requires.

If people lack knowledge of proper nutrition, they will tend to eat food that satisfies hunger immediately, but does not sufficiently nourish the body. This leads to a feeling of hunger soon after eating. Yet, the junk food aficionado doesn't realize that the reason he is hungry is that he ate junk food before. Thus, he eats junk food *again*,

---

[25] *Source*: Nerdwallet.com.

[26] J. Dickler, "Most Americans can't afford a $1,000 emergency expense," *money.cnn.com*, Aug. 11, 2011.

[27] National Center for Health Statistics. Health, United States, 2012.

providing his body with another dose of empty calories and little nutrition.

Progressivism lowers human capital by having the state take over more and more responsibility over daily life. Naturally, the individual's sense of responsibility for such tasks diminishes over time. The result is a lower level of human capital including intelligence, long-range thinking, and self-restraint.[28] Also, as the state consumes more and more of our income and wealth and imposes more and more mandates and regulatory burdens on us, our leisure time shrinks and our stress levels skyrocket. People who have been assured by progressives that the government will guarantee a safe food supply; who are too busy to make a home-cooked meal out of fresh ingredients, and who are stressed and depressed because they are tax and inflation slaves, will tend to fall prey to eating fast food and junk food, often high in sugar, that gives them a temporary rush of energy.

Diabetes is the predictable consequence of the lifestyle that progressivism has wrought. The tremendous rise in obesity has helped trigger a startling epidemic of type 2 diabetes. The American Diabetes Association defines this disease as follows:

> "Diabetes is a problem with your body that causes blood glucose (sugar) levels to rise higher than normal. This is also called hyperglycemia. Type 2 diabetes is the most common form of diabetes. If you have type 2 diabetes your body does not use insulin properly. This is called insulin resistance. At first, your pancreas makes extra insulin to make up for it. But, over time it isn't able to keep up and can't make enough insulin to keep your blood glucose at normal levels."

Doctor Mercola is correct: type 2 diabetes "is *directly caused by lifestyle.*"[29] Eating high-carbohydrate fast food and junk food and avoiding

---

[28] I am heavily indebted to Hans-Hermann Hoppe, a pioneer of human capital analysis. See, *A Theory of Socialism and Capitalism: Economics, Politics, and Ethics* (Boston: Kluwer Academic Publishers, 1989); *Democracy: The God That Failed* (New Brunswick, NJ: Transaction, 2001).
[29] "Global Diabetes Epidemic Rages On," *Mercola.com*, Dec. 5, 2011.

exercise contributes to diabetes and obesity. Recently, obesity has been shown to be a leading cause of liver disease often necessitating liver transplants.[30] The larger issue is that progressive policies systematically lower the level of human capital, including the knowledge, skill and discipline needed to maintain healthful dietary and exercise routines.

Drug overdoses. Deaths from drug overdoses have increased by three-fold since 1990 and have never been higher.[31] There is no easy explanation for this. One progressive publication said it's time for an intervention. This is puzzling as the Progressive State of America has been heavily involved in criminalizing and regulating drug use and allegedly educating the public in its government schools and elsewhere about the danger of drugs for over 100 years. If progressives were sensitive to evidence, they might have to admit that they have failed to solve this problem. Moreover, they have contributed to the problem. *Most young people are exposed to drugs when they attend government schools where drugs are ubiquitous.* Drug abuse is closely tied to anxiety, depression and hopelessness, emotions that are plentiful in a country where large numbers of people struggle to survive on a daily basis. The breakup of the family unit under progressivism surely contributes to drug abuse. The typical family used to have two parents—with the mother usually at home—monitoring their children's activities. Now, there is often one parent working one or more jobs, seeing the children just a few hours each day.

FAMILY LIFE

Daycare. In the 1960's, the typical American child was cared for during the day by his or her mother in a home where the father worked and resided. No more. In today's typical household, the mother is working outside the home and the father may not be in the picture at all or may live elsewhere. Who is taking "care" of the kids? Well, the kids are concentrated in camps called "daycare." *For the first*

---

[30] A. O'Connor, "Threat Grows From Liver Illness Tied to Obesity," *NYTimes.com*, June 13, 2014.
[31] Centers for Disease Control (2013).

time in human history, many or most of our children are being raised by strangers paid to do so.

Today, there are 11 million children under the age of five in daycare for an average of 35 hours a week.[32] Many begin their daycare career as early as six weeks old. Nauseating!

Out of wedlock births. Out of wedlock births have increased from 5.3 percent in 1960 to 40.7 percent in 2011.[33] "Nonmarital births are at higher risk of having adverse birth outcomes such as low birth weight, preterm birth, and infant mortality than are children born to married women. Children born to single mothers typically have more limited social and financial resources."[34]

EDUCATION

Progressives have controlled formal education in America for quite some time. Naturally, the results have been horrendous. The dumbing down of the country is now part of the popular culture as evidenced by Jay Leno's brilliant series of interviews showing that many Americans are ignorant of the most elementary facts. According to a recent study:

> "More than 25 percent of U.S. students fail to graduate high school in four years; only 25% of U.S. students are proficient or better in civics, as measured by the National Assessment of Educational Progress. . . 'only 22 percent of U.S. high school students met 'college ready' standards in all of their core subjects. . . Despite high U.S. unemployment, and far higher under-employment, major U.S. employers cannot find qualified American applicants to fill their job openings.

---

[32] naccrra.org/about-child-care

[33] Joyce A. Martin, Brady E. Hamilton, Stephanie J. Ventura, Michelle J. K. Osterman, and T. J. Mathews, "Births: Final Data for 2011," *National Vital Statistical Reports*, Vol. 62, No. 1 (June 28, 2013), p. 71, Table 14.

[34] S. Ventura, "Changing Patterns of Nonmarital Childbearing in the United States," NCHA Data Brief, May 2009, p. 1.

. . . 75% of U.S. citizens ages 17-24 cannot pass military entrance exams. . ."[35]

PRIVACY AND TRAVEL

The government is violating our privacy in a manner that would rival any totalitarian regime of the last century. Edward Snowden heroically blew the whistle on the Obama-approved NSA's massive illegal surveillance program that takes the eraser to the venerable 4th Amendment's ban on arbitrary searches. Amazingly, not a single Congressman filed articles of impeachment against Obama for perpetrating the largest burglary in American history. The progressive state "is everywhere; they see and hear everything . . . They observe and report your actions, your thoughts, your feelings and emotions."[36]

Federally-funded spy cams are popping up on your local street corner. We have in just the last few years lost the age-old peace of mind that comes with knowing that you are not being watched by Big Brother. Nor can we drive around without being threatened by random roadblocks that also violate the 4th Amendment. When we enter public buildings or airports, we are poked and prodded and groped and forced to take off our belts and shoes and show ID and declare where we are going.

These blanket search policies have either zero or negative security value. When you are watching everyone, you can't be watching those who really need it. These security measures could easily be defeated if any serious actor wanted to do so. *Their main function is to habituate Americans into following idiotic orders from uniformed state officers.* There was a time when Americans habitually picked up muskets when confronted by government troops barking arbitrary orders at them.

Justin Raimondo warns us: "All the elements of a police state are in place: universal surveillance, arbitrary restrictions on travel, and, most importantly, the increasingly radical and aggressive political

---

[35] J. Crotty, "7 Signs That U.S. Education Decline Is Jeopardizing Its National Security," *Forbes.com,* Mar. 26, 2012 (Study by Council on Foreign Relations).

[36] J. Smith, "It's not Just your Phone Calls – it's YOU they are Listening to," *The Daily Sheeple,* January 3, 2014.

pushback by the NSA and its supporters in Washington – up to and including the open acknowledgment that they're fully aware of the online habits of whatever members of Congress are foolish enough to get in their way."[37]

CRIMINAL JUSTICE

Incarceration. Progressive America leads the world in incarceration. "The U.S. prison population is more than 2.4 million. That number has more than *quadrupled* since 1980. That means more than one out of every 100 American adults is behind bars."[38]

This is not an accident. Progressivism is a mindset that favors the use of aggressive government force to solve social problems. Prison is one of its main tools. *Prison is the threat behind every progressive edict.* If you don't directly merit prison by violating a criminal statute, you can earn prison by interfering with a government agent enforcing progressive policies or by ignoring a court order to obey the law. A large number of prisoners are incarcerated either because they violated a progressive drug law or because their illegal drug habit drew them into a criminal lifestyle. Though statistics are hard to come by, virtually *all* state prison inmates were kidnapped by government schools from ages six through sixteen. Evidently, while there, they failed to learn right from wrong and how to make it on your own without engaging in violence or theft. I contend that government schools, being a massive exemplar of evil themselves, are incapable of teaching right and wrong.[39]

Also, the vast majority of inmates are either from poor or minority backgrounds, two groups progressives have been claiming to help for many decades through welfare policies among other ploys. In fact, welfare helped create an epidemic of fatherless families. Criminals tend to emerge from such backgrounds. After 100 years of

---

[37] "The Fight of Our Lives: The battle to beat back the NSA – and restore our old republic," *Antiwar.com*, January 6, 2013.

[38] E. Klein & E. Soltas, "Wonkbook: 11 facts about America's prison population," *Washington Post*, August 13, 2013.

[39] See, J. Ostrowski, *Government Schools Are Bad for Your Kids: What You Need to Know* (2009).

progressivism, the inner city, once a place bustling with economic activity, has become an economic dead zone. Many young people, devoid of marketable talents after being consigned to a government school warehouse for twelve years and residing in neighborhoods with few jobs, tend to drift into crime. The massive prison population of America can most definitely be traced in large part to failed progressive policies.

RACE RELATIONS

Race relations are surprisingly shaky in a country that thought it had solved its civil rights problems in the 1960s. When a black man, O. J. Simpson, accused of brutally murdering two white people, was acquitted of murder by a mostly black jury in the face of what might have been the greatest quantity of evidence of guilt ever seen in an American courtroom, many blacks cheered the verdict while many whites were flabbergasted. The latest trend in crime is the knockout game, wherein young blacks try to knock out a white person with one punch. The thugs film the event and brag about it on Facebook. Recently, a prominent black director, Spike Lee, castigated whites who moved into black neighborhoods!

African-Americans have had a raw deal *at the hands of government* throughout American history from slavery through Jim Crow and continuing under failed progressive policies such as the war on drugs. The remedy, never implemented, was to get the government off their backs and start respecting their natural right to liberty and property. Progressives took a different route, their favored approach to every problem: activist government. They would help blacks through generous welfare programs, affirmative action, loans and subsidies. This approach has failed and caused stagnation and decline in the black community. Few, however, have identified the cause, *progressivism*. The search for scapegoats ensued. Black progress is thwarted not by failed government programs but by white racism. The problems in the black community are the fault of insensitive racial remarks by TV cook Paula Dean and Duck Dynasty star Phil Robertson.

The constant scapegoating of white people for problems caused by progressivism has heightened racial tensions that increase the risk of civil unrest in the near future in America. Bottom line: progressivism, which explicitly promised better race relations if its prescriptions were followed, failed again.

SUMMARY

From 1607 through 1900, America became the greatest nation in history for average people to live and thrive. During those years, the nation was guided, albeit imperfectly, by the theory and practice of *classical liberalism*, a belief in small government and large individual freedom. That model began to change from classical liberalism to progressivism around 1900 with major policy changes coming in the early teens and continuing to this very moment. It takes time for policy changes to take full effect so the old America remained vibrant, optimistic and energetic for many decades. I recall it vividly in the 1960s.

Alas, after multiple progressive shocks such as World War I, the New Deal, and the Great Society, the nation began to stagnate in the 1970s and started palpably declining around *2001*. History, Murray Rothbard argued, is a race between state power and social power.

> "Just as the two basic and mutually exclusive interrelations between men are peaceful cooperation or coercive exploitation, production or predation, so the history of mankind . . . may be considered as a contest between these two principles. On the one hand, there is creative productivity, peaceful exchange and cooperation; on the other, coercive dictation and predation over those social relations. Albert Jay Nock happily termed these contesting forces: 'social power' and 'State power.' Social power is man's *power over nature*, his cooperative transformation of nature's resources and insight into nature's laws, for the benefit of all participating individuals. Social power is the power over nature, the living standards achieved by men in mutual exchange. State power, as we have seen, is the coercive and parasitic seizure of this production—a draining of the fruits of society for the benefit of nonproductive (actually antiproductive)

rulers. While social power is over nature, State power is *power over man*. Through history, man's productive and creative forces have, time and again, carved out new ways of transforming nature for man's benefit. These have been the times when social power has spurted ahead of State power, and when the degree of State encroachment over society has considerably lessened. But always, after a greater or smaller time lag, the State has moved into these new areas, to cripple and confiscate social power once more."[40]

What has 100 years of progressivism wrought? Each child is born with a federal debt noose around his neck. *The average American child is no longer raised primarily by his parents.* One income is no longer sufficient to support the average American family. The average American has little or no savings or cash to survive illness, unemployment, or to allow for a decent retirement.

Right around the time of 9/11, state power began to win its age-old race with social power. The evidence described above demonstrates a nation in steady decline, unlikely to be reversed unless its causes, progressivism and its policies and consequences, are reversed. To help accomplish that reversal is the purpose of this book.

---

[40] M. Rothbard, "Anatomy of the State," in *Egalitarianism As a Revolt Against Nature and Other Essays*. Washington, DC: Libertarian Review Press, 1974.

1. What is Progressivism?

"The slovenliness of our language makes it easier for us to have foolish thoughts."

—George Orwell

I told a progressive-liberal friend of mine that I planned to write a book about progressivism. He asked, "what is progressivism"? I said, "exactly!" Progressivism has been the dominant ideology in America for so long that it has been absorbed into the subconscious. We eat, sleep and breathe progressivism and hardly give it a second thought. Yet, it is this ideology that is destroying America right before our eyes.

We need to know *exactly* what progressivism is, whom its proponents are, what its origin was, what its consequences have been and what to do about it. And these questions need to be answered in a booklet that citizens—busy working to pay the taxes necessary to pay for numerous campaign promises of dead progressive politicians—have time to read.

To understand progressivism, it is necessary to understand what it replaced since progressivism was a reaction to the ideology that dominated American politics for most of its prior history. Ironically, that ideology was called by the same name that progressivism is now known to most people: "liberalism"! Historical liberalism, in its pure form, was the doctrine that favored individual liberty, voluntary cooperation and free market transactions and viewed voluntary society in the words of historian Ralph Raico as "self-generating and self-regulating."[41] The state's role in this view was merely "to defend against violent intrusion into the individual's rights-protected sphere."[42]

---

[41] "What is Classical Liberalism," *Mises Daily*, Aug. 16, 2010.
[42] *Id.*

21

In fact, liberalism as a political force was a great benefactor of humanity by helping to usher in a period of relative freedom from the ancient state and feudal kleptocracies that had plagued us from the time of recorded history. It is crucial to understand that liberalism never completely defeated the old regime. It never completely liberated humanity from state violence, force, theft and oppression that had kept us in chains for thousands of years. The progressives of the time ignored the undeniable evidence of liberalism's successes and never differentiated between problems allegedly caused by liberalism and problems caused by liberalism only winning a partial victory against the state. They complained, as they complain in all eras, that progress wasn't happening fast enough.[43] They favored using state action to improve life and increase wealth. Ironically, their method—state force—harks back to the failed methodology of the old regime, brute force. In Murray Rothbard's words, they favored using "conservative means" to achieve "liberal ends."[44] The primary difference between the old regime and the new progressive regime was progressives claimed to use force for the good of all.

The point here is this: progressivism is best understood as a reaction to liberalism. Progressivism stands for the proposition that freedom, liberty, voluntary cooperation and the free market are not enough. To best improve life, the state must intervene with men and women carrying guns and willing to use them against resistance and break up those voluntary relations and impose its will by brute force to achieve different and presumably better results. At the bottom of progressivism is a quasi-religious belief in state action (force) over individual choice.

---

[43] Cf., Ralph Raico: "Robert Skidelsky 1995: ix, defines collectivism—presumably the opposite of liberalism—as 'the belief that the state knows better than the market, and can improve on the spontaneous tendencies of civil society, if necessary by suppressing them.' He describes this as 'the most egregious error of the twentieth century...this belief in the superior wisdom of the state breeds pathologies which deform, and at the limit, destroy, the political economies based on it.'" Classical Liberalism and the Austrian School, supra at 98, n. 53.

[44] Left and Right: The Prospects for Liberty, p. 98, n. 53.

The progressive offers no plausible argument for his position. He does not and cannot proffer empirical data to support this view. And no amount of contrary evidence will change his mind! Why? Because progressivism, unlike liberalism, is not grounded in philosophy, logic, political science or economic theory. Rather, it springs from emotion or magical thinking. Just as a baby thinks he will disappear if he covers his eyes, the progressive thinks state force will improve life and believes this without evidence or logic and in the face of all contrary and obvious evidence of the failure of this approach.

For these reasons, some have called progressivism a mental illness. I prefer to view progressivism as a form of self-help therapy. The "illness" that progressive therapy seeks to cure is not necessarily a mental illness in the classic sense, but the pain and anxiety of living in a difficult, unpredictable and often hostile world where resources are scarce compared to human wants and needs and where the individual often feels powerless over events beyond his control.[45] Woodrow Wilson himself described the goal of progressivism as helping the individual to deal with forces he "cannot alter, control or singly cope with."[46]

In the face of this angst, the progressive, instead of rationally analyzing problems and finding rational solutions and paying the price demanded by such solutions, engages in wishful or magical thinking. For each problem that arises, the progressive conjures up a seemingly costless state solution. This proposal then makes progressives feel better about the world and about themselves by giving them an illusory sense of control over life. *Progressivism is a form of therapy.*[47]

This explains a lot. It explains why progressives cling to their approach in the face of contrary evidence. It explains why so many

---

[45] "[H]uman desires are insatiable, (because their nature is to have and to do everything whilst fortune limits their possessions and capacity of enjoyment,) . . . this gives rise to a constant discontent in the human mind . . ." Nicolo Machiavelli, *Discourses on the First Ten Books of Titus Livius* (1517) (Second Book).

[46] T. Throntveit, "'Common Counsel,' Woodrow Wilson's Pragmatic Progressivism, 1885-1913," in *Reconsidering Woodrow Wilson, Progressivism, Internationalism, War and Peace*, Woodrow Wilson Press, Washington, D.C., (2008), p. 25.

[47] Cf., Ludwig von Mises, *Liberalism in the Classical Tradition*, p. 15.

discussions with progressives about politics end in temper tantrums and the spewing of insults at those who disagree with them. *Progressivism isn't a rational mode of thought but a means to make the progressive feel better.* Thus, contrary evidence doesn't refute progressivism because *progressivism is not an argument* or the conclusion of an argument. It explains why progressives have an instant answer to every human problem prior to any investigation of the nature of the problem or workable solutions to the problem. *More state force is the answer to every single problem that might arise during the course of human life.* It explains why progressivism seems to be correlated with religious skepticism and declining religious belief. Whereas religious persons may seek comfort from the vicissitudes of life through their faith, nonbelievers have no similar relief valve for existential stress. Progressivism thus becomes a kind of faith for the faithless. The State replaces God. Heaven will be achieved here on earth and by means of Godvernment.[48]

Why are human beings so easily seduced by the progressive utopian vision of government action as a solution to every human problem? The harsh truth is that individual human beings are weak and vulnerable. They require food, clothing and shelter on a daily basis. They are vulnerable to disease and illness and old age. They are physically vulnerable to attack and domination by other persons and especially large groups of persons who can kill, maim or enslave them at their whim. It is true on the other hand that human beings have remarkable abilities, most importantly their intellect, to overcome these obstacles and thrive. However, all such efforts involve labor, mental and physical, and labor necessarily is unpleasant. There is a natural disinclination to work which is why, in a market society, people insist on being paid to work.

There are also two significant psychological weaknesses or vulnerabilities in people that are critical here. First, the disutility of labor applies to the process of acquiring true knowledge about politics and economics and history. People are disinclined to engage in an exhaustive study of these subjects because it is difficult and time-

---

[48] I claim no originality concerning this thesis. See, M. Rothbard, "Origins of the Welfare State in America," *Mises Daily*, Aug. 11, 2006; Voegelin, Eric (1987). *The New Science of Politics*, p. 120; Eric von Kuehnelt-Leddihn, *Leftism Revisited: From De Sade and Marx to Hitler and Marcuse*, New Rochelle, New York; Arlington House (1974), p. 54.

consuming and they would prefer to do other things with their scarce time and energy and money. This ignorance and confusion makes people vulnerable to false political solutions that nevertheless appear to be plausible on the surface. Second, people have the ability to delude themselves into believing false or baseless doctrines and to avoid facing harsh truths when doing so would appeal to their short-term self-interest or would allow them to place their own interests ahead of others. These significant vulnerabilities and weaknesses make people easy prey to political doctrines or ideologies that provide simplistic and superficially appealing solutions to life's numerous and seemingly intractable problems. Progressivism is perfectly designed to exploit all these human vulnerabilities.

Tragically, since progressivism is a false and seductive doctrine, the masses who support it not only end up *weaker, poorer and more vulnerable* than they would be without it but are deliberately drawn away from the proper solutions to life's problems: productive work, savings and investment, rational thought, careful study and research, forming positive relationships with others and engaging in voluntary cooperation with others in the marketplace and in society.

Thus, *progressivism as a form of therapy* is the best available explanation of the nature of progressivism because it explains many important facts and anomalies associated with this ideology.

In recent years, progressivism has literally served as a form of therapy for many families of victims of sudden accidental or violent death. It has become a ritual for many such families to seek to pass a law, usually named after the victim, to purportedly reduce the number of similar violent deaths in the future. After noticing a pattern of such legislative efforts, in 2009, I dubbed the practice "liberty reduction as a form of grieving." The families seek to cope with their grief by passing a law which imposes coercion on multitudes of people who had nothing to do with the death of their loved one. With liberty reduction as a form of grieving, we see the truth that progressivism is a form of therapy in its purest form.

The media is a full partner in the liberty reduction therapy phenomenon. After virtually any tragic event, they are there with the knee-jerk response of asking politicians what legislation they will propose to make sure such tragedies never happen again. They provide coverage of the lengthy process of liberty reduction from untimely death to the final bill-signing ceremony with the families and relatives present. Granted, the media has a progressive-liberal bias; however, their keen interest also reflects their estimation that their viewers or readers will also take solace from the liberty reduction efforts to make the world safe from that particular type of sudden catastrophic death.

Thus, progressivism is a mindset with a number of critical elements and premises some of which are implied and not explicitly acknowledged by the progressive himself. A mindset is "a fixed mental attitude or disposition that predetermines a person's responses to and interpretations of situations."[49] Accordingly, progressivism is:

1. a mindset about politics;
2. that has no rational basis;
3. is utopian;[50]
4. favors the use of democratic government force to solve human problems;
5. holds that government force will produce a better result than voluntary society and the market;
6. has no theory of costs, or denies or minimizes the costs of its proposed solutions;
7. is a form of self-help therapy against existential angst; and,
8. has no limiting principle and therefore tends toward creeping totalitarianism.

The following examples will illustrate how the various elements manifest themselves in actual policy debates.

K-12 Government Schools. The reaction, or rather *complete lack of reaction* to the poor performance of K-12 government schools illustrates the progressive mindset perfectly. No matter how many students lose it and shoot up the joint; no matter how much crime, violence and bullying occurs within those hallowed walls; no matter how ill-educated and ignorant the graduates are; no matter how ill-equipped for functioning in the real world they are; no matter how many teachers have affairs with their students; no prominent progressive in the public or media or political life suggests eliminating the institution itself. None ever asks if there is something intrinsically

---

[49] Thefreedictionary.com.
[50] See Chapter 8, below.

wrong with the government kidnapping our children from ages 6 through 16 and making them sit in a classroom for six or seven hours a day with children their own exact age while a civil service worker and probably a Democratic union member who got a C-average in college, purports to educate them.

The only explanation for such bizarre and irrational and *palpably cruel* behavior is the mindset of progressivism which created government schools initially when the private school system was working wonders and with zero evidence or reason to believe government schools would do better than voluntary society and plenty of reasons to believe they would not. Progressivism, as a form of emotional therapy, had no rational case for government schools in the first place so we should not expect them to have one now, or ever!

Rather, what progressives offer in the face of such failures, is not a rejection of government schools per se, which would, after all, amount to a repudiation of *progressivism per se!*, but an endless series of proposed reforms that never work because they fail to get at the root cause of the problem, the coercive element, that is, the government school element of government schools.

We see this same pattern of denial of the root cause and proposal of an endless series of failed reforms in virtually every policy area. I searched my memory for at least one progressive program that had ever been eliminated. I thought of the Comprehensive Employment and Training Act (CETA), which was repealed in 1982 after nine years of failure. However, the program was merely replaced by the Job Training Partnership Act of 1982 which in turn was replaced by the Workforce Investment Act of 1998. Job training has been a notorious and longstanding failure of progressive government, yet dozens of such programs still exist on the federal and state levels.

Thus, as a general rule, progressive programs are immortal as exemplified by the maniacal persistence of failed progressive policies on welfare, housing, employment, inflation, corporate subsidies, and illegal drugs.

Social(ism) Security. Social Security is one of the classic progressive programs. Social Security nicely illustrates two critical elements of progressivism: the fact that progressives have no theory of costs and utopianism. Their "argument" for it makes perfect sense so long as costs are ignored. Yes, it would be wonderful for all elderly people to have a steady income. Just like it would be nice if no one ever died of cancer, if all children were geniuses, and if people could fly around by flapping their arms. Of course, it does have costs, huge costs. At the beginning, as is true with the beginning of numerous progressive programs, the costs were tiny. Many paid in; only a few received benefits. The American work ethic, built up over 300 "insecure" years was still intact. Over time, more and more people were on the receiving end and fewer people were working to pay the taxes. More and more people were riding in the wagon and fewer were pulling. The program became insolvent.

At this point, as with every progressive program, there is a choice. We can pull the plug on the program and concede failure and admit that its underlying premise, progressivism, is false. Or, we can ignore the failure of the program and start down the road of endless reforms and tinkering in a vain attempt to make the program "work." Social Security has faced that dilemma 20 times and *20 times* it was decided that to save Social Security, taxes needed to be raised.[51] It turns out that Social Security does indeed have costs and the costs are enormous.

Presently, the payroll tax is 15.3% for self-employed people and 7.65% for employed people, however, the employer, using funds that from the point of view of economics properly belong to the employee, pays an additional 7.65% percent. This is an *enormous* amount of money for working class and middle class people. The "non-existent" costs are truly *enormous*. The effect of this tax is to impoverish working people to pay for the elderly who in a large number of cases need the money because they themselves were heavily taxed while they were working. The incongruous result is that many Americans are working themselves to death just to stay afloat but diners throughout America are crammed with *able-bodied* elderly flush with cash enjoying leisurely meals throughout the day.

At this point in the argument, the progressive will ask, without Social Security, how would we prevent old people from becoming poor? Liberty is the best possible answer that reason can provide. Under liberty, people have the best chance to improve their lot by working, keeping the fruits of their labors, saving without being taxed, and having access to the cheapest possible goods and services that a

---

[51] http://www.justfacts.com/socialsecurity.asp#taxes

global free market[52] can provide. There will be large sums of wealth available in such a society for private charity to help those who are still unable to make it on their own. However, even this answer will not satisfy the progressive. He will ask, what do we do about the elderly poor under liberalism?

We need to grasp the underlying premise of the question. The question assumes that there is a solution to every human problem and more specifically, there is a governmental solution to every human problem. This is utopianism, the hidden premise in the progressive mindset. (See Chapter 8). It is also a false premise. It is obvious to any honest observer that there is not a solution to every human problem. Of course, the burden of proof is on the progressive to prove that there is. No such proof has ever been or ever will be forthcoming. However, the proposition can be *disproved*. There are basic facts of the human condition and human nature that cannot be altered by the government. The laws of economics cannot be altered by government just as the government cannot alter the laws of physics or mathematics.

Efforts to use government to alleviate poverty take resources away from other sectors of the economy and cause numerous negative consequences throughout the economy. *This shift of resources itself causes poverty,* so the progressive must immediately show that the ill effects of the *new poverty* are somehow less than the ill effects of the *old poverty* now alleviated. He has never done so and cannot do so. It is impossible! Even if the knowledge problem—determining all the ill effects of the taxes spent on alleviating poverty—could be solved, and it cannot be, the progressive has no means of weighing costs to some people against benefits to others since cost is subjective to the individual and no mathematical means exists to weigh costs between and among individuals.[53]

---

[52] Note the double redundancy. The term "market" already contains within it the concepts "free" and "global."

[53] M. Rothbard, "The Myth of Efficiency," in *The Logic of Action One: Method, Money, and the Austrian School* (Cheltenham, UK: Edward Elgar, 1997), p. 266.

What is Progressivism?

Progressives argue that so-called "negative"[54] rights such as liberty are not enough, that without so-called "positive" rights such as wealth, rights are meaningless. This begs the question. The reason why there are so many poor people throughout history and currently is precisely because their negative rights and the negative rights of their parents and grandparents and fellow citizens, who might have lifted them out of poverty, were violated in the first place. This is a classic instance of indicting liberalism for the sins of its enemy the state. Throughout history, poor people, using their negative liberty, have risen to heights of great wealth whereas masses of welfare recipients have generally been mired in poverty for generations.

Government cannot alter human nature. Work is unpleasant compared to leisure. Economists call this the "disutility of labor." Raising taxes on labor will tend to reduce the amount of work people do as they are not fully compensated for their work. Paying people not to work when they reach a certain age will most definitely tend to reduce the number of people working. With fewer people working, total *wealth will decline and poverty will increase.*

Thus, utopianism, which denies all these basic facts of reality, is false. So is every progressive "argument" that relies on that premise, which is virtually every single one.

Ironically, though the progressive seeks greater control over his life through progressive programs, he ends up with far less control. Seeking control, in the end it is he who is *controlled*. Though he exercises, through voting, essentially zero control over government, progressivism grants government virtually unlimited power, always expanding, to control *him*. The levers of power in a progressive democracy are controlled not by the people, but by small, discrete, well-organized, often secretive, and ruthless groups of elites. These special interest groups, power brokers, lobbyists, and political machines invariably pursue their own selfish private interests at the expense of the rest of us. They neither know you nor care about you and in many cases are willing to literally end your very life to achieve banal policy objectives. For example, the progressive Selective Service Act of 1917 forced many men into the progressive's grand adventure, World War I, where tens of thousands of them died the most

---

[54] "Negative" because others respect your rights by doing *nothing*, that is, leaving you alone.

miserable deaths imaginable to make the world safe for Hitler and Stalin.

Worse yet, the ideology of progressivism serves as a cover for secretive private interests that seek to profit from the mass murder of modern war.[55] It should not be a surprise that an utterly irrational ideology such as progressivism would produce such bizarre results. As for democracy, as seen in the above example, it provides the common man with close to zero control over government. Voting is like trying to stop a hurricane with your breath. What is its actual function then? Democracy serves primarily as a rationalization for those who control the state to bark orders at people, backed by guns and with impunity, always with the excuse that the victim had the right to vote. To paraphrase Henny Youngman, "Take my vote, please!"

That one-liner reveals as the fraud that it is the social contract theory used by governments to justify their right to use violence against individuals. There are two main problems with the theory: it is not social and it is not a contract. Rather, it is an antisocial unilateral power grab by the state. Social contract theory is a giant and extremely destructive historical and philosophical hoax that has rationalized and justified the most heinous acts committed by government against the masses for centuries. The liberal Benjamin Constant called it "the most terrible aid to all types of despotism."[56]

Just when the older hoax that kings ruled by divine right had been refuted and discarded, a new and equally idiotic rationalization for the exercise of arbitrary power by the democratic state was invented and still plagues us. Its core notion that democratic might makes right is an essential element of the progressive mindset. But there never was a social contract. No one ever signed it and only a dolt would do so. Why would anyone agree to give up their natural rights to a state over which he exercises in effect zero control, particularly when the terms and enforcement of the contract are controlled entirely by the state itself? *The social contract may be the biggest lie of modern times.*

---

[55] See, M. Rothbard, "World War I as Fulfillment: Power and the Intellectuals," *Mises Daily*, June 09, 2007.

[56] Eric von Kuehnelt-Leddihn, *Leftism Revisited: From De Sade and Marx to Hitler and Marcuse*, New Rochelle, New York; Arlington House (1974), p. 85.

Granted that there is no explicit social contract. Does the Constitution constitute a reasonable facsimile of a social contract? *No.* No one alive today ever signed it or agreed to it when free not to do so. There are people long dead who signed a proposed Constitution and there are other people long dead who voted to ratify the Constitution. However, no living Americans ever agreed to be bound by the consent to be governed apparently made by people long dead that they did not know.

Legal scholar Randy Barnett has brilliantly refuted all possible theories of how citizens can be found to have implicitly consented to be ruled when it is perfectly obvious that they have not explicitly consented.[57] Voting does not imply consent as we never get to vote on the legitimacy of the regime itself. And what if you vote *against* the regime as I have done in every election since I was allowed to vote? How in the world can that be construed as consent? Well, I played the game. Okay, so if I stop voting, I have withdrawn my consent? That's a bargain! I will stop voting, withdraw my consent and the tax bills will cease. Hurray! Yeah, but you *could have* played the game, they will say. Barnett replies: "It is a queer kind of 'consent' where there is no way to refuse one's consent."[58] Barnett goes on to demolish all the familiar rationalizations for why average citizens have "consented" to be governed by political thugs in DC:

1. *Residency*—this argument "presupposes that those who demand that you leave already have authority over you."[59] It's a circular argument.
2. *Acquiescence to the laws.* "Does one really manifest a consent to obey the commands of someone much more powerful simply because one does not physically resist the threat of violence for noncompliance?"[60]
3. *Acceptance of the regime.* This proves too much, according to Barnett. Even oppressive regimes have the passive acceptance of their people in the sense they do not actively revolt.

---

[57] See, *Restoring the Lost Constitution* (2004), pp. 11 et seq.
[58] *Id.* at 16.
[59] *Id.* at 18.
[60] *Id.* at 21.

4. *Acceptance of benefits.* This is the most common argument made by progressives these days. With respect to the alleged benefits of the state's legal system, Barnett simply notes that there can be no consent since there is no way to opt out. The argument from receipt of tangible benefits also fails. These are paid for by compulsory taxes you never consented to. Only if such things as roads, schools, and fire protection were funded voluntarily, could you be said to have consented to the regime by using them. That never happened of course. Also, again, *to consent, there must be a reasonable way not to consent.* If I refuse to use the streets, I die of starvation. It's a distorted view of consent that leads to the "argument": join us or die!

Thus, there is no explicit or implied social contract of the kind that is implied in progressivism. The progressive's assertion that the democratic state has the right to exercise aggressive power over us[61] is instead a brute force power grab of the type human beings have been guilty of since caveman days.

* * * * *

In recent years, shrewd commentators including Lew Rockwell have noted a distinct trend towards fascism, American-style. "Fascism," Rockwell writes, "is the system of government that cartelizes the private sector, centrally plans the economy to subsidize producers, exalts the police State as the source of order, denies fundamental rights and liberties to individuals, and makes the executive State the unlimited master of society."[62] The economic aspect of fascism can be summed up as the marriage of big government and big business.

There is no inconsistency between a *progressive mindset* and a *fascist result.* Progressivism tends to devolve into militarism, economic fascism and the domination of government by special interest groups and political machines—government as cash machine for the well-

---

[62] "The Fascist Threat," *LewRockwell.com,* Oct. 6, 2011.

organized. Progressives have an uncanny knack for getting involved in major wars. See Chapter 7. Progressivism also serves as a cloak and rationalization for age-old greed and power lust. The mindset of progressivism, by giving government a blank check of virtually unlimited power, opens up a Pandora's Box containing a wide variety of dark forces that use that power for their own self-interest and often contrary to the wishes of the masses of progressives. History and theory show that the dark forces, because they can monetize their access to state power, have the economic incentive and resources to spend enormous amounts of time, energy and money cultivating power while the masses of progressives do not and cannot. Progressives asked for progress but they got fascism and corporatism instead.

Summary. This chapter has identified the specific elements and features of the progressive mindset. I do not contend that all progressives explicitly espouse or endorse these elements though they undoubtedly would concur with (4) "favors the use of democratic government force to solve human problems" and (5) "holds that government force will produce a better result than voluntary society and the market." They would likely contest the other elements and features listed. However, each of them is based on close observation and study of progressive proposals and thought over the last 100 years or is logically implied by one of the other elements. I have already demonstrated above how these elements explain actual progressive proposals and the remaining chapters will do so in even greater detail.

Thus, the first and necessary step to fixing what is wrong with America has been taken. For the first time that I am aware of in book form,[63] the elements of the mindset that is destroying America have been delineated in detail.

---

[63] A Google search failed to uncover any similar list. *Cf.,* J. Ely, Jr., "The Progressive Era Assault on Individualism and Property Rights," in Paul, Ellen Frankel; Miller, Fred D.; Paul, Jeffrey, eds., *Natural Rights Individualism and Progressivism in American Political Philosophy* (Cambridge University Press, 2012), p. 258.

2. We Are All Progressives Now

Progressivism has been the dominant political ideology of the country since about 1912 when all three candidates for President were progressives. That means the vast majority of Americans were born into a progressive world and have never known any other. I contend that if one properly understands what progressivism is—see Chapter 1—the vast majority of Americans, whether they acknowledge it or not, are progressives.

Truth is objective, not subjective.[64] If you hold progressive views, you are a progressive regardless of what you think you are or what you call yourself. For example, if you support compulsory government schools, then you must believe that government coercion can produce better results than voluntary cooperation in the marketplace, and therefore you are a progressive. Calling yourself a Republican or conservative doesn't change that fact any more than calling water "crude oil" changes the water in the slightest.

If most Republicans and conservatives were not fundamentally and ultimately progressive, we would expect to see various progressive programs eliminated or scaled back drastically when Republicans or conservatives gain power. That has rarely been the case at the federal or even state levels. *Conservative Republicans have held power over all branches of government in many states, yet not a single state has abolished government schools.* Very few progressive programs have been abolished at the federal level either. In recent years, the Republicans controlled the House of Representatives and thus, in theory, could have voted to de-fund any major program in the federal budget. Yet, no major program was de-funded.

---

[64] "What's in a name? that which we call a rose by any other name would smell as sweet." *Romeo and Juliet*, Act II. Scene II.

It can be argued that no major programs were repealed because those who opposed them feared losing elections if they did so. However, that implies that their own conservative Republican voters favored such programs or that large portions of the voting public favor such programs. At the very least, the failure to even attempt to abolish or roll back major progressive programs suggests a lack of hardcore ideological opposition to them which is consistent with at least a lukewarm progressivism.

However, the evidence of widespread progressivism among Americans is even stronger and more direct. Consider the major progressive programs: federal income tax, the Federal Reserve System, the federal welfare state, war on drugs, Social Security, Medicare and Medicaid, minimum wage laws, and extensive regulation of business. The vast majority of Americans, including Republicans and conservatives, support these programs. Republican and conservative officials consistently vote to fund and continue these programs.

Polling data bears this out. The vast majority of Americans support the core progressive programs. A recent poll showed that 80 percent of Americans want to *raise* the minimum wage.[65] 79 percent think Social Security has been good for their country.[66] On a wide range of progressive issues, polls are rare probably because pollsters perceive scant interest in abolishing this or that sacred cow such as K-12 government schools. In the absence of polls, the low vote totals of the Libertarian Party in state and local elections, from one to five percent, indicate a lack of support among the public for abolishing progressive big government. Ron Paul, the politician most opposed to progressive ideas, received a little more than 10 percent of the vote in the 2012 Republican primaries.[67] Based on that figure, we can conclude that no more than 10 percent of Americans are prepared to vote against progressive big government.

---

[65] http://nelpaction.wordpress.com/2013/07/24/new-poll-overwhelming-majority-of-americans-view-minimum-wage-increase-as-important-priority-for-congress-over-next-year/
[66] CNN/ORC Poll. Sept. 23-25, 2011.
[67] *Source*: Wikipedia.org.

We Are All Progressives Now

The fact that the vast majority of Americans hold to the philosophy that is destroying America, is of course a huge problem. Although there is widespread dissatisfaction with the direction of America and there has been for decades, there has been little recognition that the actual problem is *the political philosophy of the vast majority of Americans.* Since the opposition party, the Republicans, is itself essentially progressive, it is no surprise that this party has been utterly ineffectual in solving the problem. They *are* the problem! Or, to be more precise, they are a large part of the problem.

Electoral politics is not the only means to change government. However, there has been no effective anti-progressive movement that has pursued non-electoral strategies or tactics.

Until large numbers of people are made aware of the true cause of American decline, *their own political worldview*, there simply is no hope.

This is where we stand. We are not aware of the cause of our decline and we are not aware that our own political ideas are the cause of that decline. While this is a sad state of affairs, there is no insuperable obstacle to escaping from our predicament either.

3. The Origins of Progressivism

Progressive ideas existed well before the Progressive Era of 1900 through 1920. The most important precedent for them is Rousseau and the French Revolution. The movement for compulsory government schooling was America's first major brush with progressivism. Theodore Roosevelt, a leading Progressive Era figure, believed that Abraham Lincoln was the first progressive politician. Finally, the development of the philosophy of pragmatism around 1870 paved the way for the Progressive Era a few decades later.

French Revolution. The notion that democratic might makes right is part of the intellectual body armor of progressivism. We can trace this monstrous concept straight back to Rousseau and the first application of his ideas during the French Revolution.

Once voting is unmoored from the protection of natural rights against the state, democracy becomes simply the latest and most powerful form of tyranny. It is much easier to fight and defeat a tyrannical dictator whose regime is propped up only by force and propaganda. It has so far been *impossible* to defeat a tyranny backed by the manipulators of the majority and with the misguided and fraudulent moral cloak of democracy around it.

The modern concept of democracy is best understood in a Rothbardian framework wherein various mechanisms originally designed to limit government power are perverted and turned inside out to justify *more* government power.[68] At a time when men were ruled by kings, democracy was propounded as a check on arbitrary power and as a means to give people greater control over their own lives—more liberty in other words. Rousseau particularly, as well as

---

[68] M. Rothbard, "Anatomy of the State," in *Egalitarianism as a Revolt Against Nature and Other Essays*, Ludwig von Mises Institute, Auburn, Alabama (2nd Ed. 2000).

others, then turned democracy into an idea that gave the state virtually unlimited power so long as its officials were democratically elected.[69] This idea gives democratic government a blank check to do whatever it pleases and therefore the unlimited concept of democracy tends towards totalitarianism. The Progressives accepted this premise and reinforced it with their withering attack on natural rights, the only substantial limit on democratic prerogatives.

What limits are there to modern American government? In theory, *none* so long as democracy is the guiding principle. There are practical and economic limits of course as the system is inherently unstable and always tending towards ultimate collapse due to hyperinflation and general unrest under creeping totalitarianism.

The courts will enforce individual rights but only up to a point. That point, in my view, is this. The courts will enforce those rights such as free speech or the right to bear arms, the denial of which might lead to a collapse of the regime itself of which the judges are, of course, a part. Thus, naked self-interest serves as a modest restraint. However, as progressivism seeps ever deeper into the national subconscious, even those rights could be threatened. In recent years, most Second Amendment challenges to gun laws have failed and yet there has been hardly a whimper of protest other than a couple of large rallies in Albany, New York in 2013 and 2014. The First Amendment is also under attack as we see legislators boldly criminalizing free speech under the banner of stamping out cyber-bullying. The progressive state is like a pit bull that always advances, never retreats. Overall, the democratic state admits of few moral constraints given the burial of natural rights philosophy.

It should be noted that, as with the rest of their mindset, progressives do not present a rational argument in favor of the rightness of unlimited majority rule.[70]

Egalitarianism (Envy). Keep in mind that progressivism is largely a reaction to liberalism. Liberalism propounded a valuable theory of

---

[69] See, R. Nisbet, "Rousseau and Totalitarianism," 5 *Journal of Politics* 93 (1943).

[70] See, D. Gordon, "What's the Argument for Democracy?," *LewRockwell.com*, Jan. 25, 2005.

human equality. All human beings, including women, slaves, serfs, the poor and members of racial and religious minorities, shared the same natural rights and were entitled to equal treatment before the law as a result. This was either an entirely new idea or one that, while previously conjured, had never before been taken seriously and was certainly not made manifest in the real political world.

A different concept of equality emerges out of Rousseau's writings and the French Revolution: material equality or equality of condition or results. Equality of opportunity, though defended by many conservatives, is also a species of egalitarianism as this fuzzy concept goes beyond, and therefore contradicts the original liberal notion of equality of rights only.[71] Egalitarianism thus became the political arm of the age-old emotion of envy, the resentment of others who are perceived to have various advantages, talents or resources that the envious person lacks. As Helmut Schoeck argues in his monumental work *Envy: A Theory of Social Behaviour*, envy has always been a powerful force in society. With the French Revolution, it becomes a powerful force in modern politics as well.

In the famous slogan of the Revolution "Liberté, Egalité, Fraternité," liberty and equality are posited as prime goals of politics. If equality is understood to mean equality of natural rights, then there is no conflict between the two concepts. However, if equality means equality of results, then equality clearly tramples on liberty as the egalitarian state is continually violating the right to liberty by, for example, redistributing wealth from some people to other people.[72] While there is reason to believe that *egalité* originally meant equality before the law, over time, its meaning changed to equality of condition.[73]

Keep in mind that equality under the law per se is *not* an absolute liberal value. If a particular law, which applies only to some portion of

---

[71] Rothbard critiques the idea in *Power and Market* (Kansas City, Sheed, Andre and McMeel, 1977), p. 214.

[72] See, Robert Nozick, *Anarchy, State and Utopia*, Basic Books (1977), p. 163.

[73] See, *A Critical Dictionary of the French Revolution*, François Furet, Mona Ozouf, eds., Harvard University Press, 1989), pp. 681.

the population, violates natural rights, then the liberal would *not* support its extension to all so that the rights of all will then be violated. That is, *liberty always trumps equality under the law* when there is any conflict between the two. For example, if a law mandated that all non-Catholic parents must place their children into government school at age five, equality under the law would arguably require that Catholics also be forced to do so, however, the liberal would oppose that change in the law while advocating repeal of the original law.

It is true that there was tremendous material inequality in the eighteenth century when egalitarianism was being developed. That was not the fault of liberalism, however, which opposed the old regime that *deliberately* produced such inequality. This is another instance of liberalism being blamed for the faults of the pre-liberal regime or for problems caused by retention of large elements of the old regime even during the liberal era.

Where liberalism has been tried, the result has been a tremendous improvement in the material condition of the masses. In contrast, egalitarian regimes, whether they are of the communist or welfare state variety, have failed to improve the material welfare of the poor. Thus, liberalism, not progressivism, is the best means to improve the economic lot of the poor and the common man. What liberalism cannot easily alleviate is the envy and resentment of those who have achieved great success in the marketplace. Only progressivism can provide that tawdry service.

The tragedy of envy and the appeasement of envy through political egalitarianism is that the envious masses squander their own unique potential for achievement through pointless and self-destructive efforts to bring others down to their own level. If they applied that same energy into more positive directions through the myriad opportunities provided by the free marketplace, they could soon replace the destructive emotion of *envy* with the *thrill* of achieving goals previously thought to be impossible. As Schoeck writes, an "ideology," such as liberalism, which "inhibits envy" is "much more important to the envy-prone person, who can begin to make something of his life only when he has hammered out some sort of personal theory which diverts his attention from the enviable good fortune of others, and guides his energies towards realistic objectives within his scope."[74]

Social Gospel/Post Millennialism. Murray Rothbard has led the way in describing the enormous impact on politics of what was originally a religious movement he calls "Yankee Postmillennial Pietism."[75] This phenomenon grew out of a movement called the second Great Awakening that took place in the 1820's. Rothbard writes:

> "In the North. Especially in Yankee areas, the form of the Protestantism . . . was aggressively evangelical and postmillennialist, that is, it became each believer's sacred duty to devote his energies to trying to establish a Kingdom of God on Earth, to establishing the perfect society in America and eventually the world, to stamp out sin and 'make America holy,' as essential preparation for the eventual Second Advent of Jesus Christ. Each believer's duty went far beyond mere support of missionary activity, for a crucial part of the new doctrine held that he who did not try his very best to maximize the salvation of others would not himself be saved. After only a few years of agitation, it was clear to these new Protestants that the Kingdom of God on Earth could only be established by government, which was required to bolster the salvation of individuals by stamping out occasions for sin. While the list of sins was unusually extensive, the PMPs (postmillennial pietists) stressed in particular the suppression of Demon Rum, which clouds men's minds to prevent them from achieving salvation; slavery, which prevented the enslaved from achieving such salvation; any activities on the Sabbath except praying or reading the Bible; and any activities of the

---

[74] Helmut Schoeck, *Envy: A Theory of Social Behavior*, Liberty Press, 1969, p. 9.

[75] M. Rothbard, "Origins of the Welfare State in America," *Mises Daily*, Aug. 11, 2006

Anti-Christ in the Vatican, the Pope of Rome and his conscious and dedicated agents who constituted the Catholic Church."

Rothbard argued that this religious fervor for reform eventually became secularized and provided the initial impetus for the Progressive Movement as many of its leaders came out of PMP backgrounds.[76]

Government Schools. The compulsory "free" government school movement preceded the formal Progressive Movement by fifty years, illustrating the distinction between the formal and organized Progressive Movement (1900-1920) and the presence throughout modern history of the progressive idea—making life perfect through the use of government force.

The K-12 government school is a classic, perhaps *the* classic progressive proposal. Its proponents were not satisfied by the amazing progress being made by voluntary society and the market in the realm of formal schooling for young people.[77] Thus, the spirit of utopianism rears its ugly head and conjures up the pleasant image of an impossible perfection, a perfection to be executed by government force. *Voila*, the "free" and compulsory government school movement.

Abraham Lincoln. Theodore Roosevelt believed that Lincoln was the founding father of American progressivism. He wrote:

"[I]n the days of Abraham Lincoln [the Republican party] was founded as the radical *progressive* party of the Nation. * * * It remained the Nationalist as against the particularist or State rights party, and in so far it remained absolutely sound; for little permanent good can be done by any party which worships the State's rights fetish or which fails to regard the State, like the county or the municipality as merely a convenient unit for local self-government, while in all National matters,

---

[76] *Id.* at 200-201.

[77] See, J. Ostrowski, *Government Schools Are Bad for Your Kids* (Cazenovia Books, 2009), pp. 2-4.

of importance to the whole people, the Nation is to be supreme over State, county, and town alike.

"As to all action of this kind there have long been two schools of political thought, upheld with equal sincerity. . . . The course I followed, of regarding the executive as subject only to the people, and, under the Constitution, bound to serve the people affirmatively in cases where the Constitution does not explicitly forbid him to render service, was substantially the course followed by both Andrew Jackson and Abraham Lincoln.

****

"When I was inaugurated on March 4, 1905, I wore a ring [Lincoln's secretary, John Hay] sent me the evening before, containing the hair of Abraham Lincoln.. . . I often thereafter told John Hay that when I wore such a ring on such an occasion I bound myself more than ever to treat the Constitution, after the manner of Abraham Lincoln, as a document which put human rights above property rights when the two conflicted. . . . . I believed in *invoking the National power with absolute freedom* for every National need. . . "[78]

Lincoln can justly be called America's first progressive politician. The Civil War caused and allowed a tremendous expansion of the size and power of the federal government. It gave us our first federal conscription law, first progressive income tax, first enormous standing army; it gave us a higher tariff and greenbacks. James McPherson writes approvingly: "This astonishing blitz of laws . . . did more to reshape the relation of the government to the economy than any comparable effort except perhaps the first hundred days of the New

---

[78] *Theodore Roosevelt: an Autobiography* (New York: Macmillan Company, 1913) pp. 381-382, 394-395, 420 (emphasis added).

Deal. This Civil War Legislation . . . created the 'blueprint for modern America."[79] His program anticipates or lays the groundwork for the progressive big government that was to come. The major elements of his program included elevation of majoritarian democracy as the fundamental principle, centralization of power, a willingness to use force, including war, to achieve political goals and an enormous expansion of government's role in the economy via taxation, inflation, increased tariffs, and subsidies. Probably his major contribution to progressivism was the notion of a supposedly indivisible union which in the coming years would allow the federal government to grow to enormous size and power without fear of states seceding from the union.

Pragmatism and Progressivism. There is a very close relationship between pragmatism and progressivism as in parent to child. By pragmatism, I do not mean practicality. Rather, I mean the school of philosophy developed by Charles Peirce, William James and John Dewey from 1870 to 1907. In essence, this group developed the notion that *truth is what works.* That is, there is no truth in the traditional sense, the correspondence between our ideas and objective reality. In effect, these men, following the trend of modern philosophy, rejected the notion that there is an objective reality outside our minds that we can know. Instead, however, of explicitly rejecting the notion of truth, they simply redefined it to mean something else. They defined it out of existence. Heretofore, truth was to mean whatever we thought worked at any particular time.

Some trace the origins of pragmatism to concern over how rigid ideologies may have led to the brutal Civil War that occurred just a few decades previously.[80] However, it is a monumental intellectual error to draw a causal connection between the certainty of belief per se and violence. What causes or contributes to political violence is not certainty of belief per se but *certainty of belief in the efficacy of violence.*

---

[79] J. McPherson, *Abraham Lincoln and the Second American Revolution* (New York: Oxford University Press, 1990), p. 40.

[80] Giles Gunn, *Ideas to Die For: The Cosmopolitan Challenge* (Routledge, 2013), p. 44.

The Origins of Progressivism

Pragmatism and thus progressivism can and have become rigid ideologies themselves which come of course with their own proclivity to political violence.

Thus, pragmatism helped give birth to a self-conscious progressive ideology and movement. Progressivism became the political program of pragmatism. Pragmatism then became useful in making it appear that progressivism's ideological foe, liberalism, had no rational basis. Finally, pragmatism, with its denial of objective truth, is the ideal epistemology for progressivism, an ideology that has no rational basis in fact or logic and is, ultimately, a form of self-help therapy to make its adherents feel better about an often hostile and puzzling world.

Pragmatism also provides ammunition for progressivism's transformation of democracy from a means to choose leaders whose task is to protect natural rights to a system whose highest principle is majority rule. If we cannot know the truth, the notion of natural rights cannot be defended. What is left as our guide but the arbitrary preferences of the masses? Erik von Kuehnelt-Leddihn writes:

> "if we despair of truth, if we believe that truth either does not exist or can humanly not be attained, we either have to leave things to chance or look for mere preferences-personal preferences or 'preferences statistically arrived at' (which often means accepting the 'verdict of the majority'). This is a handy means to settle differences of opinion, yet it neither tells us the truth nor does it offer rational solutions to burning problems."[81]

In combating progressivism, there must be an awareness of how pragmatism has been absorbed into the thinking of most Americans. To slay the beast of progressivism, we must first slay its philosophical bodyguard, pragmatism. Fortunately, pragmatism is even more absurd

---

[81] *Leftism Revisited: From De Sade and Marx to Hitler and Marcuse*, New Rochelle, New York; Arlington House (1974), p. 48.

than progressivism. It contradicts itself. Assertions of truth are judged by consequences *except for the assertion of truth called "pragmatism,"* we are led to believe.[82] Like its offspring progressivism, pragmatism is an irrational worldview that is a flight from reason, logic and fact. Alas, history shows that the flight from reason usually crash-lands into the slaughterhouse.

---

[82] See, M. Crovelli, "What Empiricism Can't Tell Us, and Rationalism Can," *Mises Daily* (Jan. 26, 2006); Brand Blanshard, *The Nature of Thought*, Vol. I (1939), pp. 382-383.

4. The Failure of Progressivism

This chapter will analyze how and why the major American progressive programs and policies of the last 100 years failed. There are literally thousands of progressive programs and progressives are continually inventing and enacting new ones. It is easy to get lost in the details of multifarious progressive domestic programs and foreign wars and miss the larger point. *Progressivism was and is a reaction to liberalism.* A liberal society is one based on the natural right to liberty where people are free to do what they wish *with what they own*, their bodies and justly acquired property.

What then is a progressive society? It is one that finds the liberal society inadequate and which therefore devises an endless list of ways to *force individuals to do things they do not want to do with their bodies and their property.* In a liberal society, the individual is guided by his or her own mind. In a progressive society, the individual mind and will is gradually replaced as the guiding force by the mind and will of various government officials, politicians, bureaucrats, and police officers. If social interactions in liberalism are governed by *choice* or voluntarism, *force* is the methodology of progressivism.

Since all economic resources are scarce, no economic system can fulfill all needs and wants at the same time. Thus, it is not a fair criticism of any economic system that it fails to do so. Rather, the question is, which system is the best or better than the others at meeting human needs and wants?[83]

---

[83] The economic analysis that follows is written from what is called the Austro-libertarian point of view. No originality as to the basic ideas and principles is claimed. That perspective combines insights from the

The Failure of Progressivism

Our choices are limited, though this is obscured by the apparent availability of a variety of different economic and political systems. All such systems can be boiled down to whether they use choice or force in allocating scarce resources. They may use force or choice in varying degrees for different purposes, but it is the decision to use *choice* or *force* in various amounts which ultimately determines the kind of economic system a given society has.

In an economy based on free choice, there is a strong incentive to invest in capital and labor because the owner can then reap the rewards of increased productivity. No one can come in later when the business is making a profit and force the owner to turn over the profits. In the market, all relationships are voluntary and therefore no trade occurs unless both parties expect to benefit. The market is therefore the means by which individuals can pursue their goals in harmony with others.

In a progressive economy based on force, people will be less likely to invest in the future because of the likelihood that force will be used to siphon off the wealth so produced. Using force to take wealth from some so that it can be invested by others does not increase the total

---

Austrian School of Economics with libertarian political analysis. The following books would be helpful to those wishing to pursue these lines of thought in greater detail. Bastiat, Frédéric, "The Law," in *Selected Essays on Political Economy*, George B. de Huszar, ed. (Irvington-on-Hudson, N.Y.: Foundation for Economic Education, 1995), p. 52; Callahan, Gene, *Economics for Real People, An Introduction to the Austrian School* (Auburn, AL: Mises Institute, 2002) Henry Hazlitt, *Economics in One* Lesson (Fiftieth Anniversary Edition, San Francisco: Fox & Wilkes, 1996); Higgs, Robert, *Crisis and Leviathan: Critical Episodes in the Growth of Government* (New York: Oxford University Press, 1987) Hoppe, Hans-Hermann, *Democracy: the God That Failed* (New Brunswick, NJ: Transaction Publishers, 2002); Mises, Ludwig von, *Human Action: The Scholar's Edition* (Auburn, AL: Mises Institute, 1998 [1949]); Rothbard, Murray N., ——*For a New Liberty*, (Collier Books: New York, rev. ed. 1978); ——*Man, Economy, and State* (Auburn, AL: Mises Institute, 1993 [1962]); ——*Power and Market: Government and the Economy* (Kansas City: Sheed Andrews and McMeel, 1970).

amount of investment. It merely redirects capital from one area of the economy—the market sector—to another area—the state sector. Nor is this a zero-sum game since capital is shifted from the productive sector of the economy to the unproductive sector, destroying vast amounts of wealth in the process.

In deciding whether to use force or choice to allocate resources, we need to consider the issue of incentives. The type of system we have will affect the incentives people have to produce or not produce wealth. In a system based on choice, if people wish to improve their economic condition, their incentive will be to produce goods and services that other people will want and will choose to pay for in the market.

In a system based on force, people will generally be motivated to *produce force*, or to be part of organizations that use force to allocate economic resources. That way, they can use that force to direct economic resources to themselves. Conversely, in a system based on force, there will be a disincentive to produce goods and services because you do not have control over their distribution and cannot receive what you perceive to be their full value in any transaction. Rather, the goods and services you produce will tend to be taken from you by force in exchange for little or no compensation. Thus, economies based on force reduce the incentive of all to produce wealth and increase the incentive to produce force. Since productive work is not fully rewarded, there is an increased incentive to remain idle since leisure is not taxed. There will also be thriving black markets as people try to produce goods and services outside the reach of regulatory and tax regimes.

If we look at the peak years of Soviet Communism, a system based almost entirely on brute force, we see that the Soviets maintained an enormous and powerful army, a large and ruthless secret police force, and a huge and horrendous prison system. The Soviets invested in force because force was the coin of the realm.

In progressive mixed economies, there is still a large investment in force. Many people believe that democratic governments don't use force because the people consent by participating in elections. This is nonsense. We can see why by asking: *what are the people voting for?* They are voting to get their party into power so they can wield the levers of government force on their behalf. That is why we have three million people in the military or law enforcement. George Washington famously recognized that "government is force." Democratic force is mediated through constitutions, voting, and court decisions, but that doesn't make it any less real or violent. If people don't obey the government's edicts and laws, they will be forced to do so at gunpoint. *If they resist further, they will be shot to death with lead.*

If you look closely, you can see the enormous investments that people have made in ensuring access to the levers of force in our mixed economy: hordes of lobbyists and lawyers and pressure groups crowding our capitals and political machines totaling millions of people operating in every county and state and nationally. With government force controlling such a large portion of our economy, we have invested billions of dollars and untold human energies and time to influence the use of that force, resources that in a market economy would be freed up for much more productive pursuits.

What the *entrepreneur* is to the market, the *politician* is to the mixed economy or socialism. Both entrepreneurs and politicians purport to be problem-solvers. There is no doubt that entrepreneurs deserve that title. Just think of what Edison, Ford, and Steve Jobs have done for the world. In contrast, our most famous politicians are known for presiding over wars.

In contrast to the harmony seen in market relations, economic relationships in the progressive economy are characterized by a high degree of conflict. Whereas market transactions are voluntary and mutually beneficial, when force is used to compel transactions, the interactions become unilaterally beneficial. Indeed, it is precisely because one party does not wish to engage in a given transaction, that he must be compelled to do so. Because large numbers of persons are compelled to participate in various government programs such as government schools, those programs are usually fraught with conflict and dissatisfaction. Taxpayers, parents and students regularly attend meetings to express their dissatisfaction with the goings-on in government schools. Similar meetings of protest are unheard of with respect to the computer, software or internet industries.

Why the difference? The computer business is based on the free choice of all involved and people can use their freedom of choice to produce and purchase precisely those goods and services they desire, whereas such choice is largely absent in government schools. There, force is the predominant mode of decision making—through taxation and coercive laws and regulations. (Most regulations are taxes on non-monetary wealth.) A system based on force necessarily creates conflict as those against whom the force is used accurately perceive themselves as victims of the decision makers or as being exploited by them.

When an economy is run by force, the wishes and values of all people are not considered or even known. Prices no longer reflect actual scarcities and preferences of people; rather, they reflect the preferences of those with the power to force their preferences on others. When force is used to directly control prices, disaster ensues. Prices then no longer reflect the relative scarcity and value of goods and services. Scarce goods priced artificially low will tend to disappear and shortages will inevitably result. When prices are set artificially high, the good or service may be available but there will be a shortage of willing and able buyers.

Just as prices allow the free market to rationally and efficiently allocate resources, the general absence of market prices in government "enterprises" and for government property prevents government from doing likewise. With respect to government programs generally, Murray Rothbard explains:

> "[T]here is no way that the government, even if it wanted to, could allocate its services to the most important uses and to the most eager buyers. All buyers, all uses, are artificially kept on the same plane. As a result, the most important uses will be slighted. The government is faced with insuperable allocation problems, which it cannot solve even to its own satisfaction. Thus, the government will be confronted with the problem: Should we build a road in Place A or place B? There is no rational way whatever by which it can make this decision. It cannot aid the private consumers of this road in the best way. It can decide only according to the whim of the ruling government official, i.e., only if the government officials do the

'consuming,' and not the public. If the government wishes to do what is best for the public, it is faced with an impossible task."[84]

Summary. Economic resources are scarce. They are best allocated by their owners in freely chosen transactions in a free market. That system provides the greatest incentive to invest in the resources—land, labor and capital—needed to produce the various goods and services we call wealth. Allocating resources based on force will reduce the total amount of wealth in society and will only benefit a minority who are clever enough to gain control over the levers of power. In that system, people invest *not in capital but in force* so they can confiscate the wealth of others.

Thus, in the liberal market economy, those who wish to advance their interests are busy producing goods and services they think others will want while in the progressive economy they expend great amounts of time, energy and money getting control over the levers of government power so they can enrich themselves by means of government force such as taxation, government spending and various regulations such as those that create monopolies. The end result is that, while many people in the short run will benefit greatly from this scheme, the overall wealth of the population will be far less than it would have been in a liberal market economy.

This is easily demonstrated by analyzing the three groups involved in a key progressive policy, the government's redistribution of wealth, the government and its employees ("A"), the recipients of the largesse ("B") and forced donors or taxpayers ("C"). All three groups have a lower *incentive* to produce wealth than they would have in a free market. Further, in the case of taxpayers, they also have less *capital* which is another significant factor reducing wealth. Thus, all progressive programs that redistribute wealth—and there are hundreds of them—reduce the overall wealth available to individuals in society.

---

[84] *Man, Economy and State*, p. 820. Online at http://www.mises.org/rothbard/mes/chap12d.asp#9D._Fallacy_Government_Business_Basis

Further, the more income these programs redistribute, the greater the amount of lost wealth will be.

Another key progressive technique is regulation. Like taxation and redistribution, regulation is an extremely efficient means of destroying wealth. Regulations govern behavior or inactivity that is intrinsically harmless yet which progressives feel the need to coerce in pursuit of the illusion of control over a given alleged problem. A good example of a regulation is the requirement that unarmed security guards must be licensed, pay a fee, and undergo prescribed training.[85] Although regulations, unlike taxes, have a generally favorable image among the population, their economic impact is very similar.

While a tax is the forcible seizure of *money* by the government, a regulation is essentially a tax or forcible seizure of the individual's *property, time, energy or liberty*. Thus, regulations, like taxes, destroy wealth, sometimes with even greater efficiency. For instance, I developed an idea for a potentially international firm that would sell a certain type of useful information to consumers that is not currently available. However, when I was about to launch, I discovered several state and federal regulations barring me from starting the firm. The potential amount of wealth destroyed by these insane laws is incalculable, including in the case of my proposed business, the loss of numerous jobs in a depressed area, Buffalo, New York and the loss of a potentially valuable source of information for tens of millions of consumers worldwide.

Thus, regulations destroy an incalculable and astounding amount of wealth and the amount of wealth destroyed increases each year as the total amount of regulation increases. We lack either the tools or the imagination to grasp the amount of wealth destroyed by regulation. Perhaps the best way to imagine it is to recall how the economy functioned in the heyday of market liberalism. In his 1996 lecture, "How America Can Be Saved," Hans Herman Hoppe quoted two scholars who vividly described the favorable conditions in that era.

---

[85] Granted, such fees are the functional equivalent of taxes for purposes of economic analysis.

The Failure of Progressivism

"In 1914 Europe was a single civilized community, more so than even at the height of the Roman Empire. A man could travel across the length and breadth of the continent without a passport until he reached the frontiers of Russia and the Ottoman Empire. He could settle in a foreign country for work or leisure without legal formalities except, occasionally, some health requirements. Every currency was as good as gold, though this security rested ultimately on the skill of financiers in the City of London. . . . Nearly everywhere men could be sure of reasonably fair treatment in the courts of law. No one was killed for religious reasons. No one was killed for political reasons, despite the somewhat synthetic bitterness often shown in political disputes. Private property was everywhere secure, and in nearly all countries something was done to temper the extreme rigours of poverty."[86]

"What an extraordinary episode in the economic progress of man that age was which came to an end in August, 1914! . . . The greater part of the population, it is true, worked hard and lived at a low standard of comfort, yet were, to all appearances, reasonably contented with this lot. But escape was possible, for any man of capacity or character at all exceeding the average, into the middle and upper classes, for which life offered, at a low cost and with the least trouble, conveniences, comforts, and amenities beyond the compass of the richest and most powerful monarchs of other ages. The inhabitant of London could order by telephone, sipping his morning tea in bed, the various products of the whole earth, in such quantity as he might see fit, and reasonably expect their early delivery upon his door-step; he could at the same moment and by the same means adventure his wealth in the natural

---

[86] A. J. P. Taylor, *From Sarajevo to Potsdam*, p. 7.

resources and new enterprises of any quarter of the world, and share, without exertion or even trouble, in their prospective fruits and advantages; or he could decide to couple the security of his fortunes with the good faith of the townspeople of any substantial municipality in any continent that fancy or information might recommend. He could secure forthwith, if he wished it, cheap and comfortable means of transit to any country or climate without passport or other formality, could despatch his servant to the neighboring office of a bank for such supply of the precious metals as might seem convenient, and could then proceed abroad to foreign quarters, without knowledge of their religion, language, or customs, bearing coined wealth upon his person, and would consider himself greatly aggrieved and much surprised at the least interference. But, most important of all, he regarded this state of affairs as normal, certain, and permanent, except in the direction of further improvement, and any deviation from it as aberrant, scandalous, and avoidable."[87]

Another enormous distinction between the market economy and the ever-growing progressive economy is how each uses the unique knowledge of every individual. Market prices are the central nervous system of the economy. The price system is the means by which information about the scarcity of and the demand for resources—which information is scattered throughout the economy and otherwise not possessed by any one person—is encapsulated in one simple number: the price of a good or service. Prices fluctuate as various buyers and sellers make purchases or sales of certain goods and services and resources or abstain from making them. Prices tend toward that level which will insure that supply and demand are in balance. At that price, all those who wish to buy will have a supply of

---

[87] John Maynard Keynes, *The Economic Consequences of the Peace*, 1920, pp. 10 –12.

the good or service available. Thus, prices convey information about conditions in the world by means of a simple, easy to grasp number—the price of a good or service.

Economic value is subjective. Only individuals can truly know their values and needs and wants. Individual preferences are ranked ordinally, not cardinally. In other words, "1st, 2nd, 3rd," etc., not "1, 2, 3." That being the case, there is no way to mathematically compare one person's preferences with another's. Central planners and politicians do not and cannot know them. However, through freely chosen market transactions, individuals make their values objectively known to others, alter supply and demand and affect prices. Prices in turn then reflect the sum total of all human knowledge about the scarcity and value of economic resources. High prices lead us to conserve scarce resources while low prices tell us that the good or service is plentiful and need not be so carefully conserved. Lower-priced resources are then used to create more valuable products and commodities. Without market prices, the process of converting lower-priced goods into more valuable ones would be impossible.

Government entities whose managers do not own the capital value of their property, will, over time, have no incentive to determine the highest and best use of their properties. Thus, when government officials choose plans for how to spend government money and how to utilize government property, they are in effect choosing based on their personal preferences and values, not having any possible way of knowing what the public's priorities are. Asking the public's opinion on a survey or at a public meeting tells us *nothing* about what costs those persons would be willing to pay out of their own pockets for the projects they prefer. Thus, such commonly used approaches do not remotely replicate the efficiency of market choices.

In the progressive era, the term "free market" is poorly understood and often distorted. *The free market is simply the sum total of all voluntary economic transactions among the 7.2 billion people on the planet.* It is nothing more and nothing less. Market prices are set by the combined choices of those *billions* of people, utilizing the small bits of localized and personalized information possessed by those billions of unique individuals.[88]   In sharp contrast, in progressive economies, those decisions are made by a handful of politicians and bureaucrats. For example, the recent decision by New York State to invest over $100 million in a "green energy" company to be located in Buffalo, was probably made by about *five people* who were *not* risking their own capital.   What do these five politicians know that has eluded the collective and coordinated wisdom of 7.2 billion people, the market?

Thus, the progressive economy will feature ever-increasing taxation which destroys ever greater quantities of wealth, regulations which destroy incalculable amounts of wealth, and key economic decisions made by a very small number of politicians and bureaucrats based on their own self-interest, there being no other means of decision-making in the absence of market prices and given the subjectivity of economic value.

Aside from taxation and regulation, the progressive armamentarium has four other primary means of using force to deprive people of their natural right to liberty: war, inflation, conscription and eminent domain. That progressives have an uncanny knack for getting into wars including world wars, is an undeniable fact and important enough to merit its own Chapter 7. Progressives have instituted conscription four times and of course believe the government can do so again at its whim. Inflation was discussed in the Introduction. Eminent domain, the permanent confiscation of real estate at a level of compensation determined solely by the state was most famously used in the failed progressive program of "urban renewal."

Thus, though progressivism features a lengthy and growing list of programs and policies, *each one of them uses force to violate the individual's natural right to liberty*. The primary means of progressive force are taxation and spending, regulation, inflation, war, conscription and eminent domain. Each of these progressive tools both *destroys* and *redistributes* wealth. Redistribution, over time, reduces the incentive of each party to it, the recipient, the perpetrator and the victim, to produce wealth in the future.

---

[88] F. A. Hayek, "The Use of Knowledge in Society," *American Economic Review*. XXXV, No. 4. (1945) pp. 519-30.

The Failure of Progressivism

Only a mind infected with the virus of pragmatism (see Chapter 3)—essentially the denial that there is an objective reality that we can know—can ignore these truths and continue to run endless experiments to determine whether destroying wealth and discouraging productive work will improve society. Worse yet, for 100 years, the progressive mind has somehow failed to notice its own fatal contradiction. If there is no objective reality that we can know with our minds, how the hell are we supposed to determine if progressive policy experiments worked? And what does "worked" even mean in a world where objective truth does not exist? That progressivism turns out to be a fundamentally irrational and incoherent view of the world buttresses the case made in Chapter 1 for progressivism as a misguided form of self-help emotional therapy.

In addition to the massive deleterious economic consequences of progressive policies, as Hans-Hermann Hoppe has explained, this change in economic policy over time drastically changes the character and personality of the population and thus degrades the culture.[89] People are profoundly different in a liberal society where the predominant mode of interaction is *choice* than in a progressive one where the predominant mode is *force*.

"Civilization" is yet another term that is thrown around without a firm notion of what it means. Some definitions emphasize the element of being "advanced." However, that element fails to get to the heart of the matter as being an "advanced" society is the effect, not the cause of being civilized. I suggest that the term is better defined as containing the following elements, each of which is a precondition to being an advanced society:

- The prohibition of aggressive *violence* in dealing with others.
- The use of *reason* in dealing with others, the natural consequence of the prohibition against violence.
- The ability to imagine a better *future* and to plan for it even at the cost of immediate gratification.

---

[89] Democracy: *The God That Failed*, Transaction Publishers, New Brunswick (2001).

The Failure of Progressivism

The concept of time preference refers to an individual's preference for goods and services in the present as opposed to the future. A high time preference means a strong preference for present consumption while a low time preference indicates a willingness to defer gratification until the future. A person with low time preference is more willing to defer consumption so that investment in future production can take place. Low time preference, leading to capital investment, leading to ever increasing wealth and better technology, is what allowed to us to go from a caveman lifestyle to the digital age to the smart phone which allows you to hold in your hand access to most human knowledge.

These three concepts are inextricably linked. Only in a civilized society where violence has been banned can individuals be completely free to use their minds to advance knowledge, culture, and technology and to create the incredible variety of goods, services and products that we associate with modern life. Only where violence has been banned is the individual assured that he or she can undertake large and lengthy projects requiring significant investments of time, energy, and capital and not have all of those achievements and accomplishments stolen from him after his skull has been bashed in by barbarians whether self-employed or employed by a state.[90]

Progressivism assaults all three primary values underlying civilization. As a theory of the beneficial effects of aggressive violence, progressivism is, in Hoppe's terminology, a significant "decivilizing" force. Since the very function of aggressive force in human affairs is to negate the use of the victim's rational mind in determining how his life, liberty and property is to be utilized, *progressivism also moves society away from the use of reason in human life.* This harsh truth can be seen from the perspectives of the progressive *and* the progressive's victims. Progressives, having government guns at their disposal, need not spend time or energy developing *rational arguments* that would appeal to the minds of their victims as to the value of the various goals they wish to achieve. Government guns make that unnecessary and even silly. When is the last time you had a philosophical debate with a cop or an IRS agent?

---

[90] See, Ayn Rand, *Capitalism: The Unknown Ideal* (1966).

The Failure of Progressivism

The victim of progressive barbarism also is hindered in the full use of his rational mind. Instead of using his mind to determine how his life, liberty and property are to be utilized, he must instead be concerned with how to comply with the virtually limitless number of threats of violence progressive government aims at him. Thus, *citizens of the Progressive State of America live in a perpetual state of fear of being punished for violating edicts whose purpose either has never been explained to them or whose rationale they have never accepted or even have concluded is complete nonsense.* Worse yet, it is physically impossible for any person to even know every single law, edict, regulation or court decision that is binding upon him and virtually every such edict is vague, ambiguous or subject to serious differences of interpretation as a quick review of the Federal Reporter[91] will demonstrate.

The progressive might reply that their society is not barbaric because the violence is mainly threatened and not overt. First, this is not true. A tremendous amount of actual violence is required to keep the progressive state's edicts enforced.[92] Second and more importantly, that argument would imply that a slave plantation where the slaves were so cowered in fear of the whip that they meekly complied with the slave master's orders was the apex of civilization.

Oliver Wendell Holmes famously said, "Taxes are the price we pay for civilization." This, from a man who took part in one of the most brutal episodes in American history, the *tax-supported* American Civil War. The essence of civilization is the abolition of the use of aggressive *force* in human affairs and the consequential emergence of *reason* as our guide. *Taxation is the greatest facilitator of aggressive force ever invented.* The major wars and genocides in the tax-happy 20th century were paid for by taxation. That is why *barbarism is the price we pay for taxation.*

In addition to assaulting the very foundations of civilization, the Progressive State of America has a number of other deleterious effects on culture and character.

The institutionalized state violence that is progressivism leaks out into private behavior. The state is a powerful teacher. When it uses

---

[91] Where federal appeals court opinions are published. Many of them are dozens of pages long and beyond the comprehension of laymen.
[92] J. Ostrowski, "American Justice?," *LewRockwell.com*, Dec. 9, 2009.

force to achieve its goals, it teaches us that force is a just and efficient means of achieving our goals. The alleged fact that elections justify this force can be lost on less subtle minds. They simply see force working well for the state and they decide to use it as well. Violence can also result from retaliation against state violence as is the case with terrorism. I argued in my book *Government Schools Are Bad for Your Kids* that crime and bullying in government schools is likely the result of a reaction by the students to being forced to be in a place they don't want to be, doing what they don't want to do.

As Hoppe argues, big government reduces the overall level of human capital, meaning the wide variety of characteristics that factor into successful living. As government takes over ever more tasks of daily life, the incentive for the individual to develop the skills required to perform tasks now taken over by the state dwindles. As people become more dependent on government for wealth, information, and raising their own children, the individual's investment in supplying such goods for himself is reduced. This follows from the mere fact that labor is unpleasant. Thus, over time, people tend to become lazier, more ignorant and less able to care for their children. As Hoppe puts it:

> "[T]here will be more people producing less and displaying poor foresight, and fewer people producing more and predicting well. . . There will be more poor, unemployed, uninsured, uncompetitive, homeless, and so on, than otherwise. . . there will be less productive activity, self-reliance and future-orientation, and more consumption . . . dependence and shortsightedness."[93]

Thus, progressive government tends to make people dumber, lazier, more ignorant, more violent, more obnoxious and more infantile. See, e.g., America, circa 2014.

To sum up, the progressive toolbox contains: taxation, regulation, inflation, eminent domain, conscription and war. Progressives institute an endless series of programs of various kinds but every single one of

---

[93] Hoppe, *supra* at 32-33.

them uses these tools in various degrees and thus all of them necessarily produce negative consequences. This brings to mind the old saying, if your only tool is a hammer, every problem looks like a nail to be hammered.[94] To the progressive, a person is very much like a nail.

Each of these tools destroys wealth and lowers the level of human capital and their cumulative effect over time is to degrade the personality and character of large numbers of people.

Let us now examine in broad strokes how progressives have been nailing us for over 100 years. Progressivism's most important programs can be categorized as follows:

- Social Security
- Welfare and antipoverty programs
- Compulsory and subsidized K-12 education
- Subsidized higher education
- Socialized medicine
- Drug prohibition and regulation
- Alleged pro-labor legislation
- Occupational licensure
- Monopolization of money and regulation of banks and financial institutions
- Antitrust legislation
- Agricultural subsidies
- Job training
- Subsidies to the arts

Social Security. Like government schools (see below), Social Security is a failed program that nevertheless remains popular with the American people. Why? Keep in mind that progressivism is not a rational system of thought but a means to make progressives feel

---

[94] See, Abraham Kaplan (1964). *The Conduct of Inquiry: Methodology for Behavioral Science.* San Francisco: Chandler Publishing Co. p. 28.

better about themselves and provide a (false) sense of control over a big, complex and often hostile world. As such, the mindset necessarily excludes any notion that progressive programs might fail or might cost too much which, in the case of Social Security, is a critical issue. If progressivism was sensitive to its own failures, it would not be what it is and would not serve the purposes that make it so popular. If a program needs more resources, then, since progressives have no theory of costs or awareness that all resources are scarce, the progressive will merely propose spending more money as has been done with Social Security at least twenty times. At no time when higher Social Security taxes were proposed to save the program from insolvency, did progressives ask themselves, is this program worth the increased costs? Should we liquidate the program instead of continually increasing costs? Where are those additional resources coming from? How were those resources being used before they were taxed away? What harm will be done to persons and to their projects and to the overall economy by seizing those resources from where they are being used and applying them to save an insolvent program, the campaign promise of a dead and depraved politician, FDR?[95]

These would all be fair, rational, logical questions to ask, however, progressivism is not a rational or logical system of thought. If progressivism asked these questions, it would defeat its prime goal of making the believer feel better and have a greater sense of control over the world. It would then cease to exist in its present form!

Lest the reader think I am being too harsh on progressives, let me acknowledge that progressives do respond to allegations that their policies have failed, however, they do so by "doubling down" on progressivism. They do so in a manner that preserves the nature of progressivism as a means of maintaining a sense of control and positive emotion. They will therefore invariably propose fixing the broken, failed or insolvent program by using more government force, more taxation and more regulation. The state will get ever greater power. Social Security itself illustrates this as what was originally constructed as an inherently insolvent program with few people paying very little in, became a program with many people getting out of it

---

[95] See Chapter 9.

large sums that they never paid in. Facing the choice of liquidating an insolvent program and admitting that progressivism had failed, or doubling down on progressivism by raising taxes, the progressive chose to continue being a progressive.

So, in evaluating from a rational point of view whether the program failed, the key problem is not logical, but psychological! How do we figure out how to get our arguments and facts past the mental force field that protects the progressive from having his emotional therapy session painfully interrupted? I have no easy answer to this but believe that defining the problem itself is the first step toward solving it. Now that I hope I have the progressive's attention, what is the case for the failure of Social Security?

First, as with many progressive programs, Social Security was a classic instance of the government purporting to solve a problem caused by the failure of previous government programs. By 1935, America was not even remotely a free market nation. Big government, whose first manifestation was the Civil War (1861-1865) was now firmly ensconced in numerous areas of life and had had many decades to disrupt the workings of private society. Some of the major examples of programs that had damaged the economy included: World War I, the Income Tax, the Federal Reserve, government schools, the Smoot Hawley Tariff, Hoover's disastrous big government policies and the early portion of FDR's New Deal. All these programs destroyed private wealth, disrupted families, and reduced the wealth available to support what was a complex and successful web of private, voluntary relief agencies.[96] Worst of all was the impact of the Federal Reserve and Hoover's policies in causing, lengthening and worsening the Great Depression.

Social Security in turn immediately worsened the Great Depression:

---

[96] Alexis de Tocqueville, *Democracy in America* (1835); Richard C. Cornuelle, *Reclaiming the American Dream: The Role of Private Individuals and Voluntary Associations* (Philanthropy & society), Random House, New York, 1965.

"Payroll taxes to finance Social Security and Unemployment Insurance programs increased employers' wage bills even further, which also reduced the level of employment. In their book *Out of Work*, Ohio University economists Richard Vedder and Lowell Galloway provide econometric estimates that government-mandated payroll cost increases added nearly 1.2 million people to the unemployment rolls by 1938."[97]

Even after the Depression, Social Security increased unemployment by raising the cost of employing workers.

For those lucky enough to get a job, the payroll tax robs them of a tremendous amount of wealth for as much as 45 years in exchange for the possibility, if they remained alive and subject to the whim of Congress and *assuming that the Federal Government still existed at that time*, they would receive a modest pension paid for by extorting current workers. For those inclined to plan for the future, Social Security robs them of the capital they could otherwise invest in a market-based pension that could pay a greater rate of return. Whereas Social Security revenue is immediately spent by the state on wealth-destroying activities such as war, private pensions would be paid out of productive investment in productive assets such as stocks and real estate.

Worst of all, Social Security turns older Americans into dependents on the state, forcing them, in effect, to be cheerleaders for a corrupt, murderous, imperialistic kleptocracy just so they can be assured that the kleptocratic state will pick the pockets of younger workers to pay them a few hyper-inflated shekels in their declining years. At a time when the elderly should be relying on their families, they are forced to spend their golden years voting like automatons for the same wretched state that is destroying the future of their own children, grandchildren and great grandchildren.

"Social Security" is another Orwellian lie. It is in fact *antisocial* and *insecure*. It weakened the age-old bond between parent and child. As

---

[97] T. DiLorenzo, "A New, New Deal," *Mises Daily* (Oct. 10, 1998).

The Failure of Progressivism

Allan Carlson writes about Sweden: "The rise of the welfare state can be written as the steady transfer of the 'dependency' function from the family to the state. . ."[98] In olden days, older parents would live with their children and help raise the grandchildren. Now, adult children think nothing of moving thousands of miles away from their parents and then easing them into government-funded nursing homes where they are drugged into oblivion with Medicaid-funded drugs providing huge profits to Big Pharma. FDR and LBJ in three generations were able to undo the family structure built up over the eons. *The kids are in daycare, the grandparents are in nursing homes and the adults are tax slaves for the progressive state.* What a country!

The program is always teetering on the edge of disaster as it depends entirely on taxing current workers. Social Security is *not* an entitlement but a mere statute that can be changed any time at the whim of Congress. The level of benefits and the age of eligibility can also be changed at any time. Benefits are also subject to the vagaries of inflation and the indexing of inflation is obviously subject to manipulation. The Freudian slip on the security of Social Security is the constant refrain from Democrats that the Republicans (fat chance!) will cut your benefits if they win the next election. This is a concession of the basic *insecurity* of the program.

Of course, the government can only give what the government possesses. Thus, if the government becomes insolvent, which is the current projected trend, the checks will stop or will be paid with hyper-inflated virtually worthless dollars. Finally, if the PSA ceases to exist, *as has every other overextended imperialist power in history*, the checks will cease. Only a fool would discount that possibility in a country founded by a violent revolution, which suffered a violent Civil War and has a history of racial, religious and ethnic conflict that seems to be intensifying at the moment. If that happens, you can trade in your Treasury checks for Confederate war bonds.

---

[98] "What has Government Done to Our Families," *Mises Daily*, Jan. 5, 2003.

The Failure of Progressivism

I have argued elsewhere that the only politically practical way to abolish Social Security is to buy out current recipients with cash paid for by selling off government assets.[99]

Welfare and Antipoverty Programs. The relationship between the government and poverty is the opposite of what progressives believe. Government does not cure poverty or wage successful "wars" against it. *Government manufactures poverty and poor people.* Why is there a gulf between fact and progressive mythology? The reasons are alluded to throughout this book. Progressives are in almost complete control over the organs that transmit information and ideas about politics and have been for many decades. They have controlled the government K-12 schools for well over 100 years. In fact, they helped create them in the first place for the very purpose of touting the virtues of big government.[100] They have dominated academia for decades and since the New Deal, have bought off support from artists, writers, actors and musicians with cash bribes. All these groups, institutions and individuals have successfully made progressivism the default ideology in American politics. The opposite view, liberalism, is either not taught or is unfairly presented. It is demonized if it is mentioned at all. At the same time, the numerous flaws and fallacies of progressivism are not taught and thus are almost entirely unknown to the general public. Thus, it is not surprising that the kneejerk reaction to the problem of poverty is to propose governmental solutions.

Government causes poverty in numerous ways but here are the main factors:

- Through a plethora of laws, regulations and taxes, government makes it much more difficult, and in some cases *impossible*, for a person of modest means, or no means, to start a business. That was *not* the case over 100 years ago when penniless immigrants speaking little English could start in business by selling apples from a pushcart.

---

[99] "A $21 Trillion Tax Cut," *Mises Daily*, Mar. 20, 2001.
[100] *Government Schools Are Bad for Your Kids*, pp. 4-10.

- Through a vast complex of laws, taxes and regulations, government makes it vastly more expensive and in many cases, *impossible*, to hire new employees.

- By wasting stupendous amounts of wealth through taxation and regulation, government vastly reduces the amount of capital invested by firms. That greatly reduces productivity which is closely tied to wages.

- For those who are employed, they must pay about half of their wages in taxes.

- Further, the prices they pay for goods and services with their after-tax income are greatly increased by inflation, taxes and regulations on the firms they patronize.

These are just some of the important ways that progressive government manufactures poverty. It would take a 300-page book to provide a fair treatment of the subject.

Now, let's take a panoramic look at the effects of the government's various and endless wars on poverty. None of the antipoverty programs takes aim at the prime causes of poverty as outlined above. The vast majority simply provide cash grants to those the government defines as "poor." Predictably, paying people to be poor encourages them to remain poor longer and encourages more and more people to adjust their affairs so as to meet the definition of "poor." Over time, this has meant a titanic shift towards fatherless households as the absence of a father in the home increased the likelihood of receiving welfare.

Gradually, welfare became not a form of temporary relief from dire circumstances but a permanent lifestyle with generation after generation habituating to living off welfare. Naturally, the inclination to work and to develop and maintain the skills and habits that employers desire eroded. At the same time, progressive taxes and regulations and other policies were combining to turn the inner cities of America into economic wastelands with reduced economic opportunities.

This is where we stand today. Any honest observer not blinded by progressive ideology can plainly see that the various wars on poverty have been miserable failures and that the inner city is a place largely devoid of viable economic opportunity other than crime and drugs and prostitution where generation after generation survives on welfare and where fatherless households are now the norm. To make matters worse, crime is rampant, in large part a result of the synergistic failure of numerous progressive policies such as government schools, welfare—producing fatherless families which promotes a gang subculture, and the war on drugs. Very often there is a division of labor in this regard where females work the welfare end and males specialize in providing extra income through the drug trade and petty crime. Physically, the inner city often resembles a war zone with vacant and burned-out homes, empty blocks, long-boarded up storefronts, overgrown weeds and trees, wild animals retaking their former haunts and garbage, debris and litter everywhere. Some great society!

The war on poverty has succeeded, however, in creating a permanent class of well-paid civil servants who work in the numerous agencies that constitute the welfare state. It has also succeeded in buying off and mollifying the underclass, shut out of the highly cartelized corporate state whose big three partners, Big Government, Big Business, and Big Labor, have carved up the economy to enrich themselves at the expense of the working class and underclass.

The War on Poverty is one of the more catastrophic failures of progressivism.

Compulsory and subsidized K-12 education. This was and is the foundational progressive program. It was installed even before the formal Progressive Era by the proto-progressives of the time. As with all progressive programs, it is premised upon a belief or hope, utterly unsupported by logic, fact, evidence or experience, that in the area of educating children, the coercive state could surpass voluntary cooperation, families and the free market. As with all progressive programs, it carried with it no criteria for measuring its success or failure. And as with all progressive programs, it fails to recognize any limit on the amount of resources that should be poured into it in spite of its poor performance.

I laid out the case against government schools in my book, *Government Schools Are Bad for Your Kids: What You Need to Know (2009)*. That case is summarized in Chapter 10. It will suffice here to say that, to any honest observer, government schools have been a massive failure and truly are bad for your kids. The more important question is this: why do the vast majority of the American people refuse to accept the obvious fact that government schools have failed?

I can conjure up two main reasons. First, since most Americans are progressives, their mindset makes them largely immune to evidence or rational argument that would upset their emotional therapy masquerading as a political philosophy. The whole point of progressivism is to make the believers feel better about themselves and the world and to provide a sense of control over a big, complex and scary world. The theory does not allow for corrections based on evidence of the failure of its policies. Rather, any apparent failures are simply reinterpreted as evidence that progressivism wasn't fully executed; not enough government force was exerted; not enough taxes extracted and spent. That explains current proposals to lower the school age, make school days longer and extend the school year as well.

Second, progressives are already habituated to allowing their emotions to dictate their political views. Attacks on government schools elicit powerful emotional reactions as I have learned since I published my book. I believe the basis for the emotional reaction is *a triple-blow to the ego*. Most Americans attended government schools and sent or send their own children there. Thus, if government schools are bad for your kids, that means that their own parents sent them to a bad place; they themselves went to a bad place for up to 12 years; and they sent their own children there as well. Thus, in one blow, they may perceive an attack *on their parents* for sending them there, *on themselves* as recipients of a poor education and on *themselves as parents*.

The combined effect of the obliviousness engendered by the progressive mindset and the huge perceived blow to the ego caused by the condemnation of government schools has left most Americans in a state of stubborn denial about the horrendous state of the schools.

The Failure of Progressivism

This denial is best illustrated by the bizarre reaction to a series of mass murders in the schools. The predominant reaction has not been a questioning of the odious institution itself but a silly and mindless scapegoating of guns even though guns are already banned in schools and the shooters know that and have been encouraged by it.

There is no easy solution to waking up Americans in this regard. The first step has been taken—exposing the mindset that has so far blocked the truth from seeping into the American mind. Beyond that, I think people are being too hard on themselves and their parents. *We were all born into a progressive world not of our making.* The priority now is to make sure we don't impose this destructive philosophy on yet another generation. And it is always good to repair to the words of Emerson:

> "A foolish consistency is the hobgoblin of little minds, adored by little statesmen and philosophers and divines. With consistency a great soul has simply nothing to do. He may as well concern himself with his shadow on the wall. Speak what you think now in hard words, and to-morrow speak what to-morrow thinks in hard words again, though it contradict every thing you said to-day."

That is, it is more important for ourselves, our children and our country to admit we were wrong *yesterday* and to get it right *today* than to persist in error forever.

Subsidized higher education. Subsidizing college students is one of the sacred cows of progressivism. Progressives consider it a self-evident good and of course present no rational argument that it is worth its gigantic costs. It would be shocking if they did. Yet, this program costs billions each year and has the effect of creating student loan debt slaves of millions of Americans. The market will generally not extend credit to those who have no proven ability to pay the loan back. However, the student loan program throws money at just such people. It is hard to resist the temptation to take "free" money. This is how millions are suckered into a lifetime of debt.

At the same time, colleges have had to lower their standards to accommodate the egalitarian penchant for encouraging everyone to attend college. The value of a college degree has thus eroded, and combined with a weak economy, has left millions of college graduates unemployed or underemployed. Fast food work is common for them. In 2012, 284,000 college graduates were working at minimum wage jobs.[101]

As with socialized medicine, socialized college creates a windfall for the producers. Colleges do what any business would do with an avalanche of new money thrown at them: they jack up prices. That explains the enormous increase in college tuition in recent years which is breaking the backs of middle class families and college graduates. Many are reduced to living with their parents for years.

Like art subsidies, college subsidies are a way for the virus of progressivism to spread itself to millions of new students each year and also create a powerful, large, wealthy and sophisticated lobby for keeping and enlarging subsidies to colleges, professors, administrators and other employees.

Socialized medicine. Socialized American medicine has been a failure. It must be seen as the result of prior interventions into the medical free market that failed. Decades before the formal progressive era, doctors lobbied state governments to ban their competitors and limit the number of doctors.[102] The rationale was to protect the public; the motive was power and pelf. The similar cartelization and monopolization of nursing soon followed with the same obvious economic impact: creating an artificial shortage of nurses leading to an artificially increased price for hiring them. Finally, hospital licensing laws created an artificial shortage of hospitals and boosted their prices.

It should be noted that this massive shift of control over healing from the market to the state came at the expense of women's historical role as healers and particularly as midwives. This is an important counterexample to the prevailing progressive notion of the state as the rescuer of women downtrodden by a male-dominated society. Generations of midwives were put out of business and generations of women were forced to deal with a male-dominated medical profession

---

[101] D. Kurtzleben, "Twice as Many College Grads in Minimum Wage Jobs as 5 Years Ago," *USnews.com*, Dec. 5, 2013.

[102] H. Hamowy, "The Early Development of Medical Licensing Laws in the United States 1875-1900", *J. Libertarian Studies*, 3(1), pp. 73-119.

that frequently chose treatment methodologies that were detrimental to women's health. Women have been the victims of *millions* of government-certified unnecessary surgeries including c-sections, hysterectomies and episiotomies.[103]

These various interventions into the market, when combined with the wealth destruction caused by numerous other interventions into the market economy, increased the demand for some form of medical socialism. The progressives tried and failed many times to enact socialized medicine, however, they persisted, and Medicare and Medicaid were enacted in 1965.

These programs had two main goals that its proponents would admit to: improve health and end the two-tiered health system in which the poor were perceived to receive a lesser degree of care through charitable hospitals. The programs failed on both counts. We still have a two-tiered health care system. Because of exploding costs, Medicaid reimbursement rates have often fallen below market rates. More and more health care providers refuse Medicaid patients.

If Medicaid and Medicare had fulfilled their promise of improving the health of Americans, that fact would surely be manifest in the gross statistical measures of health collected over the last century. Yet, there is no evidence that Medicaid and Medicare had a major impact on health after they went into effect in 1966. Life expectancy and other major indicia of health were moving in a positive direction throughout the last 100 years.[104] After Medicaid and Medicare, these trends merely continued. There is little or no evidence that they improved health.

While failing to achieve its goals, socialized medicine has consumed gargantuan resources, bid up the price of medical services, greatly increased bureaucracy and regulations, and created a powerful group of special interests that constantly push for higher spending and higher taxes.

---

[103] J. Mercola, "Doctors Perform Thousands of Unnecessary Surgeries: Are You Getting One of Them?," July 10, 2013, *mercola.com*.

[104] B. Guyer, M. Freedman, D. Strobino, E. Sondik, "Annual Summary of Vital Statistics: Trends in the Health of Americans During the 20th Century," 106 *Pediatrics* 1307 (Dec. 2000).

The Failure of Progressivism

As Ludwig von Mises argued, the move toward socialized medicine created problems that led to the demand for ever more medical socialism, for example, Obamacare! There is no stable middle ground between the free market and full state socialism in health care. All middle ground programs such as Medicaid serve to pull the economy ever closer to full socialism.

We need instead to look in the other direction. We need to begin dismantling the failed model of partial medical socialism and move toward a free market in health care. We can have a free market now or we can have one later, after the inevitable collapse of fully socialized medicine.

Drug prohibition and regulation. To the liberal mind, drugs are simply private property.[105] When drugs were treated as private property, as they were throughout most of American history (through 1914), they were not a serious social problem even though you could buy "hard drugs" cheaply over the counter or by mail order. From the onset of drug prohibition in 1914, they have been a major social problem. The progressives' disruption of the natural order in this regard has been a catastrophic failure.

The state cannot effectively shut down the flow of illegal drugs in the black market. Drugs are available even in maximum security prisons. The prohibition of drugs tends to make drugs more dangerous as quality control is reduced. The ban on hypodermic needles helped spread the AIDS virus. Drugs become more potent as more potent drugs are more easily smuggled. The market for mild coca leaf tea, which Pope John Paul II drank on occasion, no longer exists in the United States. Prohibition stimulates gang violence over turf wars and, by greatly increasing the price of drugs, encourages the kind of petty theft ("car popping," shoplifting, etc.) that is common throughout the country. Illegal drugs draw in many young people with otherwise limited job prospects because of the poor education in the progressive government schools and the structural unemployment caused by various progressive policies such as the minimum wage. Most end up with criminal records that render them even more unemployable. Some end up dead or maimed in drive-by shootings.

---

[105] T. Szasz, *Our Right to Drugs: The Case for a Free Market.* Praeger, 1992.

The Failure of Progressivism

There is a massive amount of data and research condemning the drug war and not a single study which shows that its benefits outweigh its costs. My own contribution to the cause was a 60-page study for the Cato Institute in 1989 which is available online and a law review article which demonstrated the virtual impossibility of progressives ever rationally justifying their antidrug crusade.[106] In the Cato study, I noted that I wrote to every conceivable drug enforcement agency and officer and asked them for a citation to a single study that justified the drug war's existence. It was ignored of course because there is no such study. This is yet further evidence of the pseudoscientific nature of progressivism. Progressives present themselves as rational and scientific but there are no scientific studies that demonstrate the efficacy of any of their major programs. Typically for progressives, there was no pre-prohibition study of the wisdom of the crusade and no criteria for its success. They simply launched a radical change in policy and radical intervention into the free market on a whim, oblivious to the tragic consequences, the violence unleashed, the drug overdoses produced and the tens of thousands of people rotting in progressive prisons for possessing or trading private property that no one paid much attention to in the liberal 19th Century.

The progressives' efforts to regulate pharmaceutical drugs have also been a massive failure. Valuable drugs are kept off the market for years while thousands of people die waiting for them.[107] I titled my 1991 article on the FDA, "The Most Lethal Agency." Regulations vastly increase their costs and thus reduce their availability. Since government creates its own demand, increased drug prices created a demand for government-subsidized drugs. As with every subsidy program, the suppliers then jack up the price.

---

[106] "Thinking About Drug Legalization," Cato Inst. Policy Analysis No. 121 (May 25, 1989); see also, J. Ostrowski, "The Moral and Practical Case for Drug Legalization," 18 *Hofstra L. Rev.* 607 (1990); J. Ostrowski, "Answering the Critics of Drug Legalization," 5 *Notre Dame J. Law & Public Policy* 823 (1991).

[107] See, S. Peltzman, "An Evaluation of Consumer Protection Legislation: The 1962 Drug Amendments," 81 *Journal of Political Economy* 1049–91 (1973).

At the same time, regulation has the opposite effect of encouraging the consumption of too many drugs. The FDA's mission of proving that drugs are safe is absurd. Every drug including caffeine has possible negative side effects. Yet, the public is lulled into a false sense of security by the FDA. Over-prescription and overconsumption of *legal* drugs is a major problem in America. Once again, one of progressivism's marquis programs failed.

Alleged pro-labor legislation. Since the "right" of workers to *force* employers to collectively bargain with them is considered sacred, let me spell out the Misesian/Rothbardian view of the matter. Mises was not shy in his assessment:

> "[W]hat is euphemistically called collective bargaining by union leaders and 'pro-labor' legislation is . . . bargaining at the point of a gun. It is bargaining between an armed party, ready to use its weapons, and an unarmed party under duress. It is not a market transaction. It is a dictate forced on the employer."[108]

Henry Hazlitt argued that:

> "[I]f a particular union by coercion is able to enforce for its own members a wage substantially above the real market worth of their services, it will hurt all other workers as it hurts other members of the community."[109]

In his monograph, "Why Wages Rise,"[110] economist F. A. Harper compiled data showing that American wages had been rising *since 1855*, long before unions reached their peak in private sector membership in the 1940s. He also notes the close parallel between rising wages and rising productivity from 1910 through the 1950s. *Wages follow productivity*

---

[108] *Human Action: A Treatise on Economics* (Contemporary Books: Chicago, 3rd. Rev. ed., 1949) p. 779.
[109] *Economics in One Lesson* (Arlington House: New York, 1979), p. 143.
[110] The Foundation for Economic Education, 1957.

which follows capital investment. Workers who are paid substantially less than the value of what they are producing will be bid away from those chintzy firms by other "greedy" entrepreneurs who see that they can pay them more and still make a profit. In the long run, and in the economy as a whole, it is market competition and capital investment that determine wage rates. Thus, union workers gained at the expense of their non-union brethren, who were left with less capital bidding for their services, and ended up working harder for less or not working at all.

Mises points out the undeniable truth that unions are only useful to their members when they constitute a modest portion of the labor force: "unionization can achieve its ends only when restricted to a minority of workers." What good would it do to raise the wages of *all workers* by ten percent when those same workers must pay more for everything they buy to pay for everyone else's raise?

It is ironic that unions have created an image for themselves as standing up for the interests of the "little guy." The reality is that, like any other special interest group, unions obtain benefits for their own members at the expense of non-members, who make less money or who remain unemployed, and at the expense of consumers, who pay higher prices for goods and services. Unions have often allied themselves with gangsters. Unions often discriminated against racial or ethnic minorities, whom they perceived as their competition for jobs. Unions were usually allied with corrupt political machines. Isn't it time to remove the halo over unions?

Classical liberals have no objection to unions *per se*, any more than they object to other private, voluntary organizations such as the Catholic Church or the Rotary Club. They don't even object to unions engaging in actions that violate antitrust laws. If workers want to get together and *peacefully* attempt to maximize their collective economic influence, fine with them. What they object to is the fact that *the state* has given unions special legal privileges at the expense of non-union workers, businesses and consumers.

Occupational Licensure. Occupational licensure is one of the oldest planks in the progressive platform. Professionals constituted one of the most important elements of the original Progressive coalition. This illustrates the dual Dr. Jekyll and Mr. Hyde nature of progressivism with its sincere belief in government force as a positive good and its dark side: the use of the state to seize wealth, power and prestige.

The first problem with occupational licensure is competence. What evidence or logic do progressives provide to establish that the state is capable of determining who should be a doctor, lawyer or any other professional? Of course, progressives never put forth any such argument since progressivism is not a rational system of thought but a form of wishful thinking. Yet, it is clear that the state has no such competence. While the bureaucrats who issue licenses may very well be doctors or lawyers themselves, first, that does not prove that they are able to determine who should also be one. Second, those bureaucrats are chosen by elected officials who have zero expertise in either the field at issue or who should be able to work in that field. Third, those elected officials are chosen by the very public that progressives believe is incapable of choosing professionals in a free market. Yet, in the progressive regime, they must do something that is even more difficult: select elected officials who are capable of choosing bureaucrats who are capable of determining who should be licensed. It's an infinite regress of absurdity.

Much of the difficulty in licensing is determining the tradeoff between quality and price. Even if the state was able to determine a certain level of quality required for professionals, they are completely oblivious to the fact that many people will not be able to afford to hire a professional *at that level of quality*. In the free market, persons of modest means can trade off quality and price and still buy a good or service. If you can't afford a new Mercedes, you can still get a used Taurus. With licensing, you are simply barred from paying for a professional you can afford but whom the state bars from practicing due to their subjective and arbitrary judgment as to his ability.

Thus, a new problem is created: a huge number of people who now need subsidized legal, medical or other services. The progressive state then comes to the rescue after creating the problem in the first place and creates Medicaid and legal services programs. At the same time, a huge group of people are rendered unemployed by licensing laws.

Since the licensing personnel are bureaucrats with no proven ability to determine who should be a professional, it is no surprise that there are legions of incompetent professionals out there. In medicine alone, there are probably over 100,000 cases of malpractice each year.[111] Yet, the public is lulled into a false sense of security by believing that anyone with a license is competent. This is another gigantic progressive lie.

There are other negative aspects to occupational licensure. It chills free speech by professionals who can have their licenses revoked in retaliation. It decreases mobility by professionals who have to start from scratch and apply for a license in another state. And it wastes a large amount of resources consumed by the well-paid bureaucracies in fifty states now regulating as many as 500 different occupations.

Monopolization of money and regulation of banks and financial institutions. Regulation of the financial industry has always been a key feature of progressivism and it nicely illustrates the dual nature of the ideology as both an irrational and misguided but sincere belief that state force can improve human life and a cloak disguising the use of the state by special interests to seek ill-gotten gains. Progressives purport to loathe monopolies but every regulation on business reduces competition. Regulations increase costs and increased costs reduce the number of firms that can profitably operate in a given market. Licensing schemes explicitly reduce competition by legally barring firms from entering the market without a license.

The entire financial industry from the creation of fiat money by the Federal Reserve to the licensing of banks to the regulation of securities offerings to the regulation of mergers and acquisitions, is heavily regulated, licensed and controlled by the state. The practical result is to confer on *existing firms* a competitive edge against *potential competition* from firms entering the market to compete with them. Thus, progressives in this field managed to create the precise evil they claim to oppose: actual monopolies that are able to charge prices above market rates.

Antitrust legislation. Antitrust laws were one of the original progressive programs. As such, they are useful in grasping the dual

---

[111] See, J. James, "A New, Evidence-based Estimate of Patient Harms Associated with Hospital Care," 9 *J. Patient Safety* 122 (Sept. 2013).

nature of progressivism as both a sincere belief system and useful tool for special interests to seize power under false pretenses.

The theory of antitrust is that the free market will lead to industries being dominated by "monopolies" so powerful that they can "force" customers to pay higher prices than they "should." However, as Rothbard has shown, there is no way to distinguish a "monopoly price" from a "competitive price."[112] This means that progressives, while urging legal action to stop monopolies, propose no useful way to determine whether their actions have been successful. This is yet another illustration of the fact that progressivism is not a rational, fact-based or scientific ideology.

There is, however, one "business firm" that *is* a true monopoly and that *does* impose a monopoly price on its "customers" that they must pay and cannot escape. That firm is the state itself. That firm did not gain its market share by voluntary means and offering better goods and services at cheaper prices. Rather, the state gains its market share by means of brute force. Its armies drove out competing armies and its police forces and armies stand at the ready to defeat by brute force any competitor that arises. The state will in the end physically destroy you if you refuse to buy its products or resist its edicts.

Not only is the state the largest real monopoly, forcing its customers to spend about half of their income on its services, but the state also creates numerous other monopolies that plague consumers. These include all licensed institutions and professions such as utilities, hospitals, banks, transit companies, casinos, lawyers, doctors and an increasingly long list of licensed professionals and jobs. Each industry, being protected from competition by the state, then extracts higher prices than they would in a free market.

Regulation in general also involves forcing consumers to buy things they do not want and thus constitutes the very evil that progressives claim to oppose when done by the private sector.

---

[112] "In the market, *there is no discernible, identifiable competitive price*, and therefore there is no way of distinguishing, even conceptually, any given price as a "monopoly price." The alleged "competitive price" can be identified neither by the producer himself nor by the disinterested observer." *Man, Economy and State*, Ch. 10.

The Failure of Progressivism

The actual history of the drive toward antitrust laws is the exact opposite of what we are led to believe by the progressive-controlled government schools and colleges. As economist Thomas DiLorenzo unearthed in his research, the late 1800's was a time of increasing competition in the economy featuring higher production and lower prices for a wide range of critical products.[113] According to DiLorenzo, a strong case can be made that promoting antitrust law was a ruse to distract the public's attention away from the Republican Party's support for an increased tariff. Tariffs of course have the same effect as alleged market monopolies—higher prices for consumers, reduced competition and increased profits for large firms. DiLorenzo quotes the New York Times:

> "That so-called Anti-Trust law was passed to deceive the people and to clear the way for the enactment of this . . . law relating to the tariff. It was projected in order that the party organs might say to the opponents of tariff extortion and protected combinations, 'Behold! We have attacked the Trusts. The Republican party is the enemy of all such rings. And now the author of it can only 'hope' that the rings will dissolve of their own accord."

Thus, the notion that progressivism is anti-monopoly has to be considered one of the great hoaxes in political history.

Many critics of antitrust law have pointed out the hopelessly confusing nature of the doctrine and the numerous irrational and contradictory and conflicting court decisions arising out of this policy. This is as it must be since the doctrine had no rational or scientific basis in the first place. There is no scientific methodology that a court or regulatory agency can use to determine how many firms should be active in a certain market, how large they should be, how much they should produce and what prices they should set. Thus, any attempt to

---

[113] "The Truth About Sherman," *Mises Daily* (Nov. 08, 1999); see also, Gabriel Kolko, *The Triumph of Conservatism: A Reinterpretation of American History*, 1900-1916.

apply antitrust policies will be arbitrary and therefore subject to manipulation for nefarious motives such as punishing firms for political reasons and using the courts to harm competing firms that are more efficient and thus able to sell products at lower prices.

Agricultural subsidies. This is a good time to point out once again that *government creates its own demand* by creating problems that seemingly then require a governmental solution. Many of the problems the government creates arise out of war and so it is with agricultural policy. In a fascinating article, James Bovard explains that the artificial boom in agricultural production caused by subsidies during World War I created a demand for continued subsidies after the war ended.[114] This is yet another instance of war growing government domestically. *Conservatives take note.* Jim Powell further argues that government policies such as land grants and irrigation projects resulted in an over-supply of farmers.[115] Naturally, too many farmers drove down food prices leading to a demand for government intervention to cure the effects of the prior unwise interventions.

It is unfortunate that progressives fail to grasp the epistemological problem at the basis of their ideology. They simply have no idea what the consequences of their interventions into the market economy and society will be. Unwilling to acknowledge that fact, they instead plunge ahead into ever more interventions in the vain hope of ameliorating the effects of the last one while being oblivious to the future effects of the newest intervention. It's an endless chain of insanity made possible by the fact that progressivism is not a rational system of thought.

The result in this context is the usual nonsensical jumble of contradictory policies such as taxing, tariffing and regulating farmers into the poor house, then purporting to rescue them by mulcting billions from the taxpayer and handing it over to farmers, particularly the biggest ones.

---

[114] J. Bovard, "How the Feds Took Over Farming," *LewRockwell.com*, March 6, 2006.

[115] *Bully Boy: The Truth About Theodore Roosevelt's Legacy*, Crown Forum, N. Y. (2006), p. 197.

The Failure of Progressivism

Job training. Progressives have created a myriad of job training programs over the decades. All have failed, yet, since progressivism is not a rational or logical system of thought, that has not deterred them from keeping the failed old ones and starting new ones. Based on their nonsensical theory of "knowledge," pragmatism, they will apparently continue to experiment in this field to see "what works" ad infintum. Madness!

Yet, the reasons why job training fails are simple. Once you understand a few general principles, you can grasp their past failures, understand why they will fail in the future and avoid the senseless self-flagellation of endless, pointless and futile experiments in lunacy. Like every other government program, job training bureaus are *bureaucracies* and act like bureaucracies. A bureaucracy is an agency that has power over us and therefore will use that power to advance its own self-interest. Bureaucrats have little or no incentive to serve the interests of the public as their compensation is received whether or not they do so and they lack the expertise to do so even if so inclined. Running an experiment to see if a bureaucracy will cease acting like what it is—as President Obama promised after Hurricane Sandy ("no bureaucracy")—is as silly as experimenting to see if a frog will start doing calculus. Good luck and don't let a million failed experiments deter you because, hey, you never know!

The original goal is never achieved but the program inevitably becomes a racket, a source of income for bureaucrats and government contractors. This illustrates what can be called the three laws of progressivism:

- Every progressive program will fail to achieve its stated purpose but will achieve a secondary and unstated and nefarious purpose, to enrich and empower discrete public sector and/or private sector interests at the expense of the rest of us.
- The material beneficiaries of the failed program will lobby the government to continue it in spite of its failure.

The Failure of Progressivism

- The tenacious ability of failed progressive programs to cling to life is explained by the interaction of the progressive's irrational belief in government force as the solution to every human problem and the omnipresence of special interest groups that benefit from these failed programs.

Subsidies to the arts. While most progressive programs at least take aim at real problems, subsidizing artists appears to be a solution in search of a problem. It is hard to believe that before uber-progressive FDR first proposed subsidizing artists, there was a widespread clamoring for such a program: "Hey, we have a serious problem. We have to buy up all the art nobody wants." In the absence of any apparent problem in this regard, to find an idealistic motive for art subsidies, we must repair to the general policies underlying progressivism. We can, however, exclude *egalitarianism* since subsidizing a special class of people for pursuing their presumably enjoyable hobby hardly seems fair or egalitarian. Art subsidies, however, fit well within the general framework of progressive utopianism as an area of life that purportedly can be made better through government action. As usual, however, this progressive program has all the usual flaws: no theory of costs, no criterion for the success of the program and thus, of course, no way to conclude *from a progressive point of view* that the program failed!

There are more specific problems: how to define art, define quality art, and determine which art should be subsidized? What gives government the competence to do so? The non-artist in government must necessarily choose those who staff the art agencies while the philistine voters choose the non-artists. Won't subsidies be used to advance the political agenda of the politicians and thus corrupt and distort art itself? There are so many questions that progressivism cannot answer since it is not a rational system of thought!

The one undeniable use of art subsidies is a goal never advertised or promoted initially: the art world is now firmly in thrall to progressive big government. "Whose bread I eat, his song I must sing."

5. Progressivism's Archenemy— True Liberalism

Probably not one in 10,000 Americans knows that the blue and buff colors of the Continental Army were chosen because they were previously the colors of the old British Whig Party, one of the first liberal political parties.[116] The idea was George Mason's, the Father of the Bill of Rights. Most Americans haven't the slightest clue about what historical liberalism was, who its heroes were, what its magnificent accomplishments were, what the world was like before liberalism, or how it basically created America and made it the best country in history for people to live their lives. Neither do they know why it declined and how it was replaced and with what. Since *progressivism* replaced true or historical liberalism and is now destroying the country, this colossal ignorance is obviously a huge problem.

None of this should be a surprise in a country where ninety percent of the population is "educated" in progressive government schools which are essentially daytime juvenile detention and political brainwashing facilities. Compounding the problem is the loss of the word "liberal" as it is now taken to mean *progressive*, the opposite of its original meaning. Worse yet, the small and ineffectual political party which roughly speaking espouses the historical liberal viewpoint, goes by a different term, "Libertarian." As pointed out later in the book, this unfortunate neologism, among other problems, serves to cut off the modern movement from its glorious past since its past heroes were

---

[116] Don Troiani, James L. Kochan, Earl J. Coates, James Kochan, *Don Troiani's Soldiers in America, 1754-1865*, (1998), p. 52; Ron Chernow, *Washington: A Life*. Penguin (2010), p. 174.

not known by that term.[117] We need to make the liberal tradition come alive again if we are to have any hope of reversing America's decline and we need to recapture the word "liberal" and restore its original meaning.

Throughout most of recorded human history, life for the common man was marked by its brevity and poverty and by violent exploitation. Slavery, serfdom, and other forms of subjugation were the norm. A standard model was conquest of a people, expropriation of the lands and forcing the conquered people to work the land for subsistence wages or their equivalent, with most of the profits being skimmed off by the rulers.[118]

Liberalism partially overthrew the old regime with results best described by Ludwig von Mises in 1929:

> "[B]rief and all too limited as the supremacy of liberal ideas was, it sufficed to change the face of the earth. A magnificent economic development took place. The release of man's productive powers multiplied the means of subsistence many times over. On the eve of the World War . . . the world was incomparably more densely populated than it had ever been, and each inhabitant could live incomparably better than had been possible in earlier centuries. The prosperity that liberalism had created reduced considerably infant mortality, which had been the pitiless scourge of earlier ages, and, as a result of the improvement in living conditions, lengthened the average span of life. . . . On the eve of the World War the worker in the industrial nations of Europe, in the United States, and in the

---

[117] Chapter 10.

[118] Franz Oppenheimer, *The State: Its History and Development Viewed Sociologically* (New York: Vanguard Press, 1926); Albert Jay Nock, *Our Enemy the State* (Tampa, Fl.: Halberg Publishing Corp., 2001; Murray Rothbard, *Ethics of Liberty* (Atlantic Highlands, N. J.: Humanities Press, 1982), pp. 162-72.

overseas dominions of England lived better and more graciously than the nobleman of not too long before. . . . It was precisely in the countries that had gone the farthest in adopting the liberal program that the top of the social pyramid was composed, in the main, not of those who had, from their very birth, enjoyed a privileged position by virtue of the wealth or high rank of their parents, but of those who, under favorable conditions, had worked their way up from straitened circumstances by their own power. The barriers that had in earlier ages separated lords and serfs had fallen. Now there were only citizens with equal rights. No one was handicapped or persecuted on account of his nationality, his opinions, or his faith. Domestic Political and religious persecutions had ceased, and international wars began to become less frequent. Optimists were already hailing the dawn of the age of eternal peace."[119]

Like progressivism, liberalism was a set of ideas before it began to affect policy. The "first self-consciously libertarian mass movement" was the Levellers, part of the Republican faction in the English Civil War around 1648-49.[120] Rothbard writes, "the Levellers, led by John Lilburne, Richard Overton, and William Walwyn, worked out a remarkably consistent libertarian doctrine, upholding the rights of 'self-ownership,' private property, religious freedom for the individual, and minimal governmental interference in society. The rights of each individual to his person and property, furthermore, were 'natural' — that is, they were derived from the nature of man and the universe, and therefore were not dependent on, nor could they be abrogated by,

---

[119] *Liberalism In The Classical Tradition*, Translated by Ralph Raico, Foundation for Economic Education, Inc. Irvington-on-Hudson (3rd Ed. 1985), pp. 1-2.

[120] An Austrian Perspective on the History of Economic Thought, Vol. I, p. 313.

government."[121] The Levellers did not immediately affect policy, however, because they were violently suppressed by Cromwell. Some of them were executed.

The Levellers influenced the leading British liberal thinkers of the late 17th Century and early 18th Century including Algernon Sidney, John Locke, and Trenchard and Gordon of *Cato's Letters*. According to Rothbard, "each made a profound contribution to the growth and development of libertarian thought in America."[122] Sidney was one of the first to advocate a natural right to liberty, "natural" meaning, among other things, *existing prior to and independently of government.*[123] He was also one of the first to posit a right of revolution against tyrannical government.[124]

John Locke is the most famous of the liberals largely because of his influence on Jefferson's Declaration of Independence. Locke argued for what at the time was a simple but startling conclusion: each man had ownership of his own self. He also had a natural right to own property. Government's sole function was to protect these rights. If it did not, the people had the right to overthrow the government through revolution. One can see here the basic theory of the Declaration through Locke's influence on Jefferson. Rothbard sums up Locke's thought as follows: "Locke, by the use of reason in investigating the laws of man's nature, adumbrated the doctrine of the natural rights of the individual to person and property, rights that are anterior to government and that government is duty-bound to defend, on pain of a justified overthrow."[125]

Several decades later, two pamphleteers, John Trenchard and Thomas Gordon helped spread liberal ideas in both Great Britain and America through their widely read Cato's Letters. Rothbard writes:

---

[121] *Id.*

[122] Murray N. Rothbard, *Conceived in Liberty*, Vol. II, p. 188.

[123] See, G. Galles, "More on Algernon Sydney," *Mises.org*, Nov. 19, 2004.

[124] *Conceived in Liberty*, *Vol. I*, p. 686.

[125] *Id.* at 689.

Progressivism's Archenemy— True Liberalism

"*Cato's Letters* . . . greatly radicalized the impact of Locke's libertarian creed. They did so by applying Lockean principles to the concrete nature and problems of government, in a series of powerfully argued and hard-hitting essays that were often cited and reprinted and widely read throughout the American colonies. *Cato's Letters* did more than merely restate Lockean doctrine. From the position that the people have the right to revolt against a government destructive of liberty, 'Cato' proceeded to argue with great force that government is always and everywhere the potential or actual aggressor against the rights and liberties of the people. Liberty, the source of all the fruits of civilization and human happiness, is ever liable to suffer the aggressions and encroachments of government, of power, the source from which war, tyranny, and impoverishment ever flow. Power always stands ready to conspire against liberty, and the only salvation is for the public to keep government within strictly limited bounds, and to be ever watchful, vigilant, and hostile to the inevitable tendencies of government power to encroach upon liberty. . . . The American colonists eagerly imbibed from Trenchard and Gordon, not only the Lockean doctrine of individual liberty and of the right of revolution against government in what Professor Bernard Bailyn has justly called a 'superbly readable' form; but also, and even more important, the dichotomy between liberty and power, and the ever-constant threat to the crucial liberties of the people by the eternal incursions and encroachment of governmental tyranny."[126]

---

[126] *Conceived in Liberty*, Vol. 1, p. 693.

Progressivism's Archenemy—
True Liberalism

These liberal theorists gave humanity several extremely important concepts that apparently did not exist previously, or if they did, had not come to public awareness:

- First, the right of self-ownership. One would think that humanity would have noticed this concept sooner. Alas, we owe this critical discovery to the liberals.

- Second, the right to own property, derived from the right of self-ownership.

- Third, that rights are *natural*, that is, inherent in the nature of things and not bestowed by government. They are a higher law to which positive law or government law must give way in any conflict between the two.

- Fourth, that people have the right to revolt and overthrow governments that systematically violate natural rights.

Whether or not that last concept had been thought of before, it was liberals who cogently argued for it and publicized it at a time when they could have lost their lives for doing so. In fact, in 1683, Algernon Sidney did die for his espousal of liberal views. He was tried for treason and executed for upholding the right of revolution. The chief witness against him was his own treatise, *Discourses Concerning Government (1680)*.

Sidney's fate was not unusual for early liberals. Their radical challenge to the powerful led to the systematic persecution of liberals in England by the government. According to George Smith:

> "Many received lengthy prison terms in barbaric, premodern dungeons and many were brutally executed. It's worth noting in this context that no group has been more critical of 'cruel and unusual punishment,'

mistreatment of prisoners and the death penalty than liberals. They certainly know whereof they speak."

The early liberals discovered the natural right to liberty which can be defended against government by force if necessary. Combining the rights of self-ownership and property, liberty can be defined as *the right to do what you wish with what you own*. Nor does liberty need exceptions or adjectives such as "ordered" or "peaceful." *Peace and order are already contained within the concept of liberty*. Liberty is necessarily both peaceful and orderly and nothing else is or can be.

Later generations of liberal thinkers added to the doctrine by noting the ability of individuals in society to coordinate their activities without dictates from a central authority. According to historian Ralph Raico:

> "Historically, where monarchical absolutism had insisted that the state was the engine of society and the necessary overseer of the religious, cultural, and, not least, economic life of its subjects, liberalism posited a starkly contrasting view: that the most desirable regime was one in which *civil society—that is, the whole of the social order based on private property and voluntary exchange—by and large runs itself*. For at least a century and a half, the idea that society and the state are rivals, that social power is diminished as state power grows, has been typical of those recognized as—or accused of—being the most 'dogmatic,' 'doctrinaire,' and 'intransigent' of the liberals."

> "Since liberalism is essentially a doctrine of society's self-regulation—of its capacity to generate beneficial spontaneous order—a special role falls to economic theory, the best developed branch of social-scientific knowledge that has investigated phenomena of spontaneous social order. . . . society is taken to be essentially an incalculable network of ever-changing

voluntary exchanges. . . . Most succinct is the Physiocratic slogan, '*Laissez-faire, laissez-passer, le monde va de lui-même*' ('the world goes by itself')."[127]

Liberalism was more than just an intellectual movement. It was an extremely effective and important political movement across the Western world.

Freedom of Religion. Throughout history, freedom of religion was lacking and wars of religion were common. The liberals solved this problem by urging religious freedom and tolerance. Professor Raico writes:

> "Liberalism scored a major victory with the attainment of religious toleration (often for prudential reasons) and, finally, religious freedom, as it came to be acknowledged that in this area civil society could be left to fend for itself."[128]

Industrial Revolution. The Industrial Revolution lifted mankind out of the mud, the muck, the despair and the insect, vermin and disease-ridden hovels, shacks, huts and caves of the previous eons. It liberated us from slavery and serfdom and drudgery. Children in progressive government schools are taught that it was a period of great evil only to be cured by progressive big government policies. The progressives' lies about the Industrial Revolution amount to one of the greatest defamations of all time. Wendy McElroy writes:

> "From the 18th through the 19th century, the world surged forward in technology, industry, transportation, trade, and life-changing innovations like cheap cotton clothing. Within two centuries, the worldwide per capita income is estimated to have increased tenfold and the population six fold. The Nobel Prize–winning

---

[127] *Classical Liberalism and the Austrian School*, 2012, pp. 98-99.
[128] *Id.* at 94.

economist Robert Emerson Lucas Jr. stated, 'For the first time in history, the living standards of the masses of ordinary people have begun to undergo sustained growth . . . Nothing remotely like this economic behavior has happened before.' The dramatic advance in prosperity and knowledge was achieved without social engineering or centralized control. It came from allowing human creativity and self-interest to run free at a glorious gallop. Abuses certainly occurred. Some can be laid at the door of governmental attempts to harness the energy and profits of the period. Other abuses occurred simply because every society includes inhumane or amoral people who act badly, especially for profit; this is not a criticism of the Industrial Revolution but of human nature."[129]

War and Peace. Before liberalism, war was generally assumed to be an inescapable part of the human condition. War has even been touted for having alleged beneficial effects on the economy. *Liberals pioneered antiwar analysis.* This will surprise many who view classical liberals as extreme right-wingers and who deem antiwar sentiments as the exclusive province of the political left. Liberals argued, for example, that economic protectionism can lead to war as states feel the need to gain by force what has been closed off to them by trade restrictions.[130]

For centuries, liberals critiqued war, bemoaned its costs, explored its causes, and exposed its beneficiaries and those who secretly plotted for war. Professor Ralph Raico writes in *Great Wars and Great Leaders: A Libertarian Rebuttal:*

> "For generations, the unmasking of such excuses for war and war-making has been the essence of *historical*

---

[129] "Redeeming the Industrial Revolution," *Mises Daily*, Nov.17, 2011.
[130] See, George Smith, "American History, Part One" video lecture, http://www.youtube.com/watch?v=7p4S9TuT08c.

revisionism, or simply *revisionism.* Revisionism and classical liberalism, today called libertarianism, have always been closely linked."[131]

According to Professor Raico these liberal antiwar heroes included: Richard Cobden, John Bright, Herbert Spencer, Lysander Spooner, William Graham Sumner, Gustave de Molinari, Albert Jay Nock and H. L. Mencken.

The traditional liberal foreign policy was non-intervention and neutrality. This was recommended by Washington and Jefferson and expounded more recently by the modern libertarian tradition. The point is not that we think foreign states are sacrosanct. Murray Rothbard, in particular, thought most were murderous kleptocracies.

Rather, the case for non-intervention is based on hard-nosed realism:

- Non-intervention tends to keep foreign disputes narrow and localized. World wars, with their inevitable globally disastrous consequences, are avoided.

- Classical liberals deny that such as Stalin, Clinton, Churchill, Wilson, Roosevelt, Truman, Johnson and Nixon, already busy violating the rights of their own subjects, have any training, experience or competence, in coming to the rescue of those whose rights are being violated by their own hack politicians and dictators. These gentlemen's humanitarian rescue missions resulted in Hitler taking power in Germany, Eastern Europe being enslaved by communism, genocidal chaos in Southeast Asia, bombing Serbia back to the Stone Age, millions upon millions of civilian and military casualties, and the current mess in the Middle East.

---

[131] Ludwig von Mises Institute, 2010, p. vii.

Progressivism's Archenemy—
True Liberalism

- Foreign intervention leads to "blowback" (the CIA's term). In the words of Frederic Bastiat, people are not clay; they always react and respond to the state's use of power against them in ways that result in unintended and negative consequences from the state's point of view. The dim-witted state is like a chess player who is unaware that the other fellow gets to move after he does. The widespread use of state power erodes private morality, as people learn from the state's actions and rationalizations that it is acceptable to use force against others to achieve their goals. These two factors are the foundation of modern terrorism.

- An interventionist state is a large, powerful, and snooping state. It has a large standing army, inconsistent with the traditional republican reliance on a citizen militia. It requires heavy taxation to support the military bureaucracy and tends towards repression of civil liberties since the warfare state cannot brook dissent.

- Domestic policy comes to mirror foreign policy. The warfare state leads inexorably to the welfare state as the apparent success of military central planning leads to demands for domestic central planning. Thus, from those who think society should be run like an army barracks, we get the "war on poverty" and the "war on drugs".

Abolition. The abolition of slavery was a complex, gradual development for which no one individual, philosophy or group can claim sole credit. However, Christians and liberals were among the earliest critics of slavery.[132] John Locke condemned slavery in his Two Treatises of Government:

> "Slavery is so vile and miserable an Estate of Man, and so directly opposite to the generous Temper and Courage of our Nation; that 'tis hardly to be conceived, that an Englishman, much less a Gentleman, should plead for't."[133]

It is unsurprising that the only political philosophy founded on the individual's right of self-ownership, condemned chattel slavery. (Granted, all mainstream philosophies including progressivism, condemn chattel slavery, however, each endorses substantial violations of the right of self-ownership and all endorse the taxing away of the fruits of one's labor by force, a form of retroactive forced labor.) Chris Berg explains, "Central to Locke's thought was a belief in natural rights—the rights of life, liberty and property which were inviolable, and that governments were formed to protect, not undercut. An antislavery position was unavoidable if you believed in natural rights."[134]

Free trade. The early 20th Century liberal Albert Jay Nock accurately viewed tariffs as the robbery of the domestic consumer by the domestic manufacturer.[135] Another aphorism, attributed to liberal thinker Frederic Bastiat, graphically stated another powerful reason to establish free trade: "If goods don't cross borders, troops will." Historian Jim Powell explains that in the free trade era in the late 19th century:

---

[132] C. Berg, "How Christians & classical liberals defeated slavery," http://www.ipa.org.au/sectors/ideas-liberty/publication/2198/how-christians-classical-liberals-defeated-slavery

[133] *Two Treatises on Government*, Book I, page 1.

[134] *Id.*

[135] "Anarchist's Progress," *Mises Daily*: Sunday, Oct. 14, 2007.

Progressivism's Archenemy—
True Liberalism

"There was unprecedented freedom of movement for people, goods, and capital. By reducing intervention in economic affairs, governments reduced the risk that economic disputes would escalate into political disputes. There wasn't much economic incentive for military conquest, because people on one side of a border could tap resources about as easily as people on the other side of a border. Trade expanded, strengthening the stake that nations had in the continued prosperity of one another as customers and suppliers. While free trade was never a guarantee of peace, it reduced the danger of war more than any public policy ever had."[136]

Liberal economists led the way towards free trade. Trade created interdependence among countries that not only led to rising living standards among the masses but also discouraged war by reducing the incentives for war and by creating interdependencies among countries.[137] France and Great Britain fought each other for centuries until liberals helped engineer a trade agreement between the two countries in 1860. Peace has prevailed ever since.[138]

Free speech and habeas corpus. Like religious freedom, recognition of the right to free speech is almost entirely a liberal accomplishment. In four of Cato's Letters, Trenchard and Gordon set forth their views of freedom of speech. As Jonathan Emord writes:

"Trenchard and Gordon believed free speech 'essential to free Government.' They perceived a property in

---

[136] Quoted in G. Galles, "Richard Cobden: Activist for Peace," *Mises Daily*: Feb. 5, 2003.

[137] D. Griswold, "Peace on Earth? Try Free Trade among Men," *Cato.org*, Dec. 28, 2005.

[138] G. Breiger, "Trade Trumps War: How two ancient enemies turned away from more bloodshed," *Antiwar.com*, Mar. 6, 2000.

one's speech and also understood the rights of property
and speech to 'always go together.'"[139]

Trenchard and Gordon identified three central values that the right of
free speech is designed to advance. First, freedom of speech allows
people to criticize the government and make it more responsive to
popular will. Second, freedom of speech is necessary for the pursuit of
truth in science and art. Third, freedom of speech is essential for
individual self-fulfillment and expression.

By the time Thomas Jefferson wrote to James Madison in 1787, it
was accepted by the leading political thinkers in America that freedom
of speech and of the press were natural rights belonging to each
citizen. Jefferson, away in France, chastised his protégé Madison for
failing to include a bill of rights in the Constitution which should
include, among other provisions, "freedom of the press." Madison,
then a congressman, drafted a bill of rights, drawing heavily upon the
Virginia Declaration of Rights that was the work primarily of anti-
Federalist George Mason. Madison's First Amendment, modified in
various ways of no great importance to us now, became the law of the
land in 1791.

Having been ratified, the First Amendment seemed to attract little
attention for the next 126 years. The Amendment did not stop the
Federalists from enacting the Alien and Sedition laws in 1798 which
outlawed speech critical of the government. Thus, in ten short years,
the wily Federalists went from arguing that no First Amendment was
necessary because the federal government was not delegated any power
over the press, to arguing that the federal government could regulate
political speech even after the passage of the First Amendment.

Jefferson, typically, saw the contradiction. He wrote to the naive
Madison, who had seen no need for a First Amendment:

---

[139] *Freedom, Technology, and the First Amendment*, Pacific Research Institute
for Public Policy, 1991, p. 31.

Progressivism's Archenemy—
True Liberalism

"Among other enormities, [the Sedition act] undertakes to make certain matters criminal tho' one of the amendments to the Constitution has expressly taken printing presses, etc., out of their coercion."[140]

Much of American history can be seen as an on-going debate between the liberal Jefferson and the proto-progressive Lincoln and this is true on the issue of free speech. In 1839, the liberal Alexis de Tocqueville had written:

"Among the twelve million people living in the United States, there is not one single man who has dared to suggest restricting the freedom of the press."[141]

Just twenty-five years later, Lincoln, true to his Federalist and Hamiltonian[142] roots, felt no compunction whatever about jailing during the Civil War a total of thirteen thousand civilians who had expressed pro-Southern views. According to historian Arthur Ekirch, this was often done "without any sort of trial or after only cursory hearings before a military tribunal."[143]

Another twist on the Lincoln-Jefferson dichotomy is their respective positions on habeas corpus. Jefferson complained that the "eternal and unremitting force of the habeas corpus laws" was not protected in the new Constitution. Lincoln in contrast, illegally suspended habeas corpus during the Civil War and simply ignored an order by the Chief Judge of the Supreme Court to release a political prisoner. Franklin Roosevelt also showed callous disregard of habeas

---

[140] Letter to Madison, June, 1798.

[141] *Democracy in America*, Vol. 1, Part II, Ch. 3.

[142] For evidence of Hamilton's direct influence on Progressivism, see Herbert Croly, *The Promise of American Life*, New York: Bobbs-Merrill Company, Inc. (1965), pp. 38, et seq.

[143] Arthur A. Ekirch, *The Decline of American Liberalism*, New York: Atheneum, 1980, pp. 124-125.

corpus by imprisoning Japanese-Americans during World War II with the approval of a thoroughly progressive Supreme Court.

The next time free speech was challenged during wartime was World War I. During that war, run by a progressive president, Woodrow Wilson, Congress passed the Espionage Act of 1917, which forbade among other things, promoting insubordination or refusal of duty among the armed forces. Three persons convicted under this Act appealed their convictions to the Supreme Court, arguing that their activities were privileged and shielded from prosecution by the First Amendment. In these cases, the illegal behavior consisted of publishing a pamphlet opposing the draft, publishing a pamphlet sympathetic to Germany, and speaking out in favor of socialism.

Had the three defendants, including Eugene V. Debs, been judged by a Supreme Court sympathetic to the natural human right of free speech, their convictions would certainly have been overturned. History, however, played a cruel trick on them. The judge assigned to write the opinions of the court in all three cases was thoroughly Hamiltonian and progressive and was the most vociferous critic of natural rights theory America has ever seen—Oliver Wendell Holmes.

Holmes had nothing but scorn for the man who first insisted that a free speech amendment be added to the Constitution: Thomas Jefferson. On the one hundredth anniversary of John Marshall taking the bench as chief judge of the Supreme Court, 1901, Holmes made reference to Jefferson's political enemy and cousin. He spoke of:

> "the fortunate circumstance that the appointment of Chief Justice fell to John Adams, instead of to Jefferson a month later, and so gave it to a Federalist and loose constructionist to start the working of the Constitution."

Then he obliquely noted that:

> "Time has been on Marshall's side, and the theory which Hamilton argued, and [Marshall] decided, and

Webster spoke, and Grant fought, and Lincoln died, is now our corner-stone."[144]

I say "obliquely" because Holmes never states just what that "theory" is that is now our corner-stone. Whatever that "corner-stone" is, however, it is safe to assume that Holmes thought Jefferson's philosophy was now buried under it.

Is this the man you would want judging your First Amendment case, with ten years in prison at stake? In a famous essay entitled "Natural Law," the prototypical progressive Holmes tells us in stark terms just what he thinks of the natural rights philosophy that underlies the First Amendment:

> "There is in all men a demand for the superlative, so much so that the poor devil who has no other way of reaching it attains it by getting drunk. It seems to me that this demand is at the bottom of the philosopher's effort to prove that truth is absolute and of the jurist's search for criteria of universal validity which he collects under the head of natural law."[145]

Rejecting natural law, Holmes gives us his own progressive theory of law: it is "the majority will of that nation that could lick all others," a legal philosophy that is not surprising coming from an officer in the Union Army in the Civil War.

What does this odd man do with the three defendants who claim to have been speaking freely? Typical for a pragmatist, he creates out of thin air his own law of free speech:

> "We admit that in many places and in ordinary times the defendants would have been within their constitutional rights. But the character of every act depends upon the circumstances in which it is done.

---

[144] "John Marshall," in *Collected Legal Papers*, pp. 87-91.
[145] "Natural Law," *Harvard Law Review* (1918).

The most stringent protection of free speech would not protect a man in falsely shouting fire in a theater and causing a panic. [The] question in every case is whether the words used are used in such circumstances and are of such a nature as to create a clear and present danger that they will bring about the substantive evils that Congress has a right to prevent. It is a question of degree and proximity. When a nation is at war many things that might be said in time of peace are such a hindrance to its effort that their utterance will not be endured so long as men fight, and that no Court could regard them as protected by any constitutional right."[146]

Based on this clear and present danger doctrine, the court upheld all three convictions.

Holmes was finally put in his place by a contemporary who was even more cynical, more sarcastic and more brilliant: the great liberal H. L. Mencken. In a review of a collection of Holmes' dissents, Mencken wrote:

"In the three Espionage Act cases, one finds a clear statement of the doctrine that, in war time, the rights guaranteed by the First Amendment cease to have any substance, and may be set aside by any jury that has been sufficiently inflamed by a district attorney itching for higher office. . . . I find it hard to reconcile such notions with any plausible concept of liberalism. . . . If I do not misread his plain words, he was actually no more than an advocate of lawmakers. There, indeed, is the clue to his whole jurisprudence. *He believed that the law-making bodies should be free to experiment almost ad libitum*, that the courts should not call a halt upon them until they clearly passed the uttermost bounds of reason, that everything should be sacrificed to their

---

[146] *Schenck v. United States*, 249 U.S. 47, 52 (1919).

autonomy, including, apparently, even the Bill of Rights. . . . Like any other man, of course, a judge sometimes permits himself the luxury of inconsistency. Mr. Justice Holmes, it seems to me, did so in the Abrams case, in which his dissenting opinion was clearly at variance with the prevailing opinion in the Debs case, written by him. But I think it is quite fair to say that his fundamental attitude was precisely as I have stated it."[147]

Ironically, and largely by accident as Mencken suggests, Holmes' clear and present danger doctrine, originally used to provide the government with the power to regulate political speech during wartime, became the basis for later case law which offers much protection for political speech that urges unpopular or even illegal acts, except where such advocacy "is directed to inciting or producing imminent lawless action and is likely to incite or produce such action."[148]

The present-day formulation of the clear and present danger doctrine has resulted in a substantial amount of protection for free speech. However, as the three World War I cases demonstrate, what constitutes a "clear and present danger" will differ from judge to judge, often because of the political and philosophical views of the judge. Progressive judges who are hostile to the philosophical basis of the right of free speech—natural rights—and to the values that right promotes, could at any time shift First Amendment doctrine back to the days when speaking out against the draft could land one in jail for ten years.

That is why it is important to understand the history and philosophy of the First Amendment. It is important to understand that the First Amendment is historically and philosophically a Jeffersonian and liberal creation, an expression of the natural rights of the

---

[147] "Mr. Justice Holmes," in *The Vintage Holmes*, A. Cooke, Ed., New York, Vintage Books, 1955, p. 189, et seq (emphasis added).
[148] *Brandenburg v. Ohio*, 395 U.S. 444, 447 (1969).

individual against the state; that as such it is in continual danger of being abrogated and interpreted out of existence by the progressives whose uncanny knack for achieving political power is the direct result of their love of that power.

Equal rights for women. It will come as a shock to those who incorrectly view libertarians as extreme right-wingers to learn that their ideological ancestors, the liberals, pioneered women's rights. In Social Statics (1851), a work derided by the progressive Holmes in his dissent in *Lochner v. New York*, 198 U.S. 45 (1906), Herbert Spencer wrote a chapter on "The Rights of Women" the overall thrust of which no libertarian would contest:

> "Equity knows no difference of sex. In its vocabulary the word *man* must be understood in a generic, and not in a specific sense. The law of equal freedom manifestly applies to the whole race—female as well as male. The same *à priori* reasoning which establishes that law for men (Chaps. III. and IV.), may be used with equal cogency on behalf of women. The Moral Sense, by virtue of which the masculine mind responds to that law, exists in the feminine mind as well. Hence the several rights deducible from that law must appertain equally to both sexes." (Chapter XVI).

Natural rights versus civil rights. Note that while the scope of natural rights is limited, *progressives don't believe in natural rights at all.* Their *civil* rights are purely the creation of legislation and can be changed at any time since they are based on nothing but air.[149] Further, they are not

---

[149] For example, Conor Williams believes that rights "are judged by their consequence, by their fruits." That judgment is no doubt to be made by the majority through elections. Since rights are determined by the subjective judgments of the majority and "mean different things in different historical contexts", there are in effect, no rights at all in the progressivism system. See, "Defending Progressivism," *Dissent*, Sept. 7, 2010.

rights at all since they involve aggression against others as they generally involve *forced* association. In contrast to the current perception, the package of natural rights proposed by liberals, life, liberty and property, and equal treatment *by government* in all matters, is vastly more beneficial than the civil rights package offered by progressives. What good are civil rights which allegedly guarantee non-discrimination in society if the state taxes most of your income, regulates every aspect of your behavior and conscripts you to fight in a foreign war in which you are killed?[150] The list of natural rights is short but the rights themselves are powerful, valuable and necessary. The package of civil rights proffered by progressives *in place of* natural rights is long but mainly serves to shield the individual from the hurt feelings that can result from people exercising the natural right of free association while offering no protection against the most dangerous threat to any individual: the violence of the state.

Liberalism protects the smallest minority in the world, *you*, from an infinite variety of physical abuse by the state. To progressives, you are merely an unknowable and meaningless micro-statistic whose rights and interests can be sacrificed away in the arbitrary judgment of some degenerate politician whose thirst for power is achieved by auctioning off your life, liberty and property in exchange for the votes of the greedy and depraved. Mencken was correct:

> "The state—or, to make the matter more concrete, the government—consists of a gang of men exactly like you and me. They have, taking one with another, no special talent for the business of government; they have only a talent for getting and holding office. Their principal device to that end is to search out groups who pant and pine for something they can't get, and to promise to give it to them. Nine times out of ten that promise is worth nothing. The tenth time it is made

---

[150] See, Henry Mark Holzer, "The Constitution and the Draft," 6 *The Objectivist* No. 10 (Part I) and No. 11 (Part II) (1967) (with Erika Holzer).

good by looting A to satisfy B. In other words, government is a broker in pillage, and every election is a sort of advance auction sale of stolen goods."[151]

Liberals understand that *you* are, in the words of Nietzsche, ". . . something unique, and that no accident, however strange, will throw together a second time into a unity such a curious and diffuse plurality . . ."[152] You had your own unique plans for the funds the politicians auctioned off against your will and there is no rational or moral means to conclude that the *loss to you* of the means to fulfill your aims is somehow justified by the alleged *gain by the recipient* of the stolen goods. Robert Nozick explains this brilliantly:

> "[T]here is no *social entity* with a good that undergoes some sacrifice for its own good. There are only individual people, different individual people, with their own individual lives. Using one of these people for the benefit of others, uses him and benefits the others. Nothing more. What happens is that something is done to him for the sake of others. Talk of an overall social good covers this up. (Intentionally?) To use a person this way does not sufficiently respect and take account of the fact that he is a separate person, that his life is the only life he has. *He* does not get some overbalancing good from his sacrifice, and no one is entitled to force this upon him-least of all a state or government that claims his allegiance (as other individuals do not) and that therefore scrupulously must be *neutral* between its citizens."[153]

---

[151] "Sham Battle", *Baltimore Evening Sun*, Oct. 26, 1936.
[152] "*Schopenhauer As Educator*," in Walter Kaufmann, ed., *Existentialism From Dostoevsky To Sartre* (World Publishing Co., 1956), pp.101-104.
[153] *Anarchy, State and Utopia*, Basic Books (November 11, 1977), p. 32-3.

Progressivism's Archenemy—
True Liberalism

Opposition to Conscription. Once again, opposition to the military draft is often perceived to be a left-wing point of view. However, here is yet another instance where liberals spoke out for the long-neglected rights of a persecuted minority lacking political power, young men in wartime. Historian George H. Smith writes:

> "The Englishman Thomas Hodgskin [served] as a cadet aboard a British warship. . . . Hodgskin . . . after which he wrote *An Essay on Naval Discipline* (1813), a scathing indictment of conscription and the brutal conditions endured by British sailors. Hodgskin's experience with the horrific punishments inflicted on British sailors for even minor offenses caused him to question both the justice and utility of the supposed 'right' to punish. British sailors, who typically hailed from lower-class backgrounds, were frequently pressed into service against their wills, and their officers tended to view them as brutes who could be controlled only by the lash. Hodgskin, who by this time had read John Locke, William Paley, and other moral philosophers, had a different opinion. Humans, created by God with 'similar passions,' are 'everywhere made alike.' Many individual differences are caused by different social and political environments. If the English tended to be happier and more virtuous than people from other nations, this was largely because they were less governed than other nations. And if English sailors appeared more brutish than other Englishmen, this was owing not to any inherent defects in their natures but to the barbarous conditions of naval life. In short, if you treat men like brutes, they will behave like brutes. Press gangs and conscription, according to Hodgskin, should be abolished and replaced by voluntary, short-term enlistments; pay should be increased so that sailors can afford a decent standard of living; and the draconian penal laws of the navy — which were

applied arbitrarily, without recourse to due process —
should be eliminated. If there must be punishment,
then the navy should follow the example of the civilian
courts in England, which 'do not punish the innocent'
and which are administered according to impartial laws,
not by the whims of superiors."[154]

In sharp contrast to the liberals' condemnation of soldier slavery,
progressives have enthusiastically endorsed the concept. Progressives
reject the entire notion of natural rights including the right of self-
ownership. To them, all rights are granted by the state in its sole
discretion. Progressives combined to enact the Selective Service Act of
1917, designed to assist the progressives' war to make the world safe
for democracy, World War I. The statute was enacted by a progressive
Congress, signed by a progressive president, Woodrow Wilson, and
upheld by a progressive Supreme Court whose members included two
rabid progressives, Holmes and Louis Brandeis.

One of the few victories of the modern Liberty Movement was
sparked by the efforts of a little-known libertarian tucked quietly away
in the Nixon White House, Martin Anderson. Anderson, almost
single-handedly engineered the end of the military draft in 1971.[155] No
statue in his honor has yet been erected.

Right to bear arms. We have seen many times what happens when
citizens or subjects are defenseless against tyrannical regimes—mass
murder. R. J. Rummel has documented the gloomy and massive body
count in numerous scholarly works including, *Death by Government.* The
right to bear arms is perhaps the most important of the natural rights
as its denial can and has led to immediate violent death. If you lack the
tools needed to defend yourself against tyrants and criminals, the other
natural rights are rendered meaningless.

Gay rights. Gays have the exact same natural rights as every other
person, no more and no less. That includes, life, liberty, property and

---

[154] "Thomas Hodgskin: Libertarian Extraordinaire, Part 1," *Libertarinism.org,*
May 29, 2012.
[155] L. Rice, "The Persuasion of Nixon," *AtlasSociety.org.*

free association, which is implied in the second and third rights. On the other hand, *like everyone else*, they lack the right to force anyone to associate with them or the right to impose "contractual" relations on others by the force of law. It is no surprise that classical liberals were among the first writers to advocate for the rights of gays.[156]

Bill of Rights. The liberal contribution to the Bill of Rights was enormous. Many of the core ideas are derived from or are at least consistent with the liberal notion of natural rights. Though many of the enumerated rights are *procedural* rights, the right to be secure from arbitrary searches combines procedural and substantive natural rights while free speech, religious freedom, and "life, liberty and property" are pure *natural* rights. The Ninth Amendment, which protects unremunerated rights, was also clearly intended to incorporate natural rights into the body of the Constitution.[157]

Freedom of travel. In the progressive era, the right to travel is slowly being destroyed. Ron Paul's quip that we had better worry that the fence being built along the Mexican border might one day be used to prevent us from leaving was only a shock to those who can't project trends. Once we were free to travel. Then, *thanks to the progressives*, we needed government permission, passports.[158] Then, they restricted taking cash out of the country. Then, they restricted travel to certain countries.

In better times, freedom of travel was one of the major accomplishments of the liberals. Professor Jane McAdam's 2011 survey of the history of the idea rightly gives classical liberals their due in pioneering the right:

---

[156] R. Raico, "Gay Rights: A Libertarian Approach," *Libertarianism.org* (1975).

[157] See, R. Barnett, "The Ninth Amendment: It Means What It Says," 85 *Tex. L. Rev* 1-82 (2006).

[158] W. McElroy, "Where Are Your Papers," *The Daily Reckoning*, Nov. 7, 2011.

"[I]n his writings on the social compact between the state and its citizens, John Locke (1632–1704) regarded leaving one's country as the means by which one could refuse consent to be part of a political community (since, in his view, governance required such consent). In Locke's view, the right to expatriate oneself was a manifestation of self-governance and individual self-determination. . . . Jefferson . . . described emigration and independence as a natural right, bolstering American claims to the right to expatriation, which would enable a severance of links to the British Crown: '[O]ur ancestors, before their emigration to America, were the free inhabitants of the British dominions in Europe, and possessed a right, which nature has given to all men, of departing from the country in which chance, not choice, has placed them, of going in quest of new habitations, and of there establishing new societies, under such laws and regulations as, to them, shall seem most likely to promote public happiness.' Further, he stated: 'I hold the right of expatriation to be inherent in every man by the laws of nature, and incapable of being rightfully taken from him even by the united will of every other person in the nation.'"[159]

As always, the liberals pioneered an important human right which is now slipping away thanks to progressives. The liberals understood that we needed this right to escape the myriad forms of tyrannical government. In the 20th Century, the denial of this right led to the murder of millions by their own governments.

---

[159] "An Intellectual History of Freedom of Movement in International Law: The Right to Leave as a Personal Liberty," *Melbourne Journal of International Law* (2011), pp. 11-13.

Progressivism's Archenemy—
True Liberalism

Historical Timeline

The Old Regime: 3500 B. C. to 1650

Era of Liberalism: 1650-1900

Era of Progressivism: 1900-2014

Multicultural tolerance and peace. One of the great virtues of liberalism is that, it alone among the political worldviews, discovered a way for people from different ethnic, racial and religious groups to live together in relative peace. In all systems of powerful government, including progressivism, *these groups struggle with each other for control of the state.* As I demonstrated in a paper presented at the Mises Institute in 2002, the major cause of war in the last fifty years was conflict between or among competing ethnic, racial and religious groups *inside* states: civil war.[160] *The state system has not only failed to solve the problem of peace among disparate groups but in fact is itself the major cause of conflict and violence among these groups.* The cause of the violence is the fear of or the actual exploitation and domination of ethnic, racial or religious groups *by a state* controlled by hostile groups.

It is also a myth that the best way to smooth over multicultural differences is through the ballot box. *This is false.* The ballot box is simply a means to determine how *state violence* is to be used against the losers of the election and how those losers will then be exploited economically and in other ways by the majority. Thus, the incentive for minority groups to attempt to secede or seize control of the state to avoid such domination and exploitation exists in democracies and dictatorships. In 23 of the 25 recent intrastate wars, the prevailing regime was democratic throughout the dispute or at least at certain times during the dispute.[161] In certain cases, a democratic government

---

[160] "The Myth of Democratic Peace: Why Democracy Cannot Deliver Peace in the 21st Century," *LewRockwell.com*, Feb. 19, 2005.
[161] *Id.*

was overthrown *because of* the feeling of an ethnic or religious subgroup that its interests were not being protected or advanced by the democratic state.

Thus, in strong states that exercise a great deal of control over people's economic and personal lives, groups that do not control the state live in constant fear of exploitation, domination, and sometimes genocide itself. In such states, whether democratic or not, different groups live in continual fear that competing groups may increase their political power, including by increases in population and immigration and thus, *the state creates a conflict of interests that would not otherwise exist!* In a liberal market society, disparate groups and individuals may live side by side, house to house, without the slightest fear that those who differ from them will seize control of the state and deprive them of their life, liberty or property. They may associate with them if they wish, trade with them to their mutual benefit if they wish, *or not* associate with them if that is preferred. Most importantly, peace is achieved!

It must be emphasized that progressive government, contrary to popular myth, *exacerbates racial, ethnic and religious tensions* and does not ameliorate them. Every progressive policy, involving as it does state violence, creates winners and losers and thus resentment among the losers. Thus, the progressive's favored policies such as civil rights laws (forced association), affirmative action (affirmative racism) and welfare; create winners and losers and therefore resentment among the losers. Under liberalism, both parties in every voluntary transaction are winners and positive relations among different groups are attained.

Multiculturalism and big government are a toxic mix. We see this today all over the world with ethnic, racial or religious violence ongoing in Iraq, Ukraine, Syria, Sudan, Israel/Palestine, Darfur, Chechnya and other regions. Those who look forward to a peaceful multicultural world should embrace liberalism and the free market. No other political system can maintain peace and tolerance in a multicultural world.

This brief survey of the magnificent accomplishments of liberalism illustrates the huge gulf between the achievements of the historical liberty movement and the extremely poor image the public has of the contemporary Liberty Movement. If the Movement had hired a public relations firm to poison the public mind about us, the results would be similar. We are a bunch of kooks; a bunch of Don Quixoties whose ideas have had no impact on the world; we all live in Mom's basement; we are Ayn Rand cultists; we are racists, anti-Semites and gay-bashers; we are champions of the interests of billionaires and plutocrats and large multinational corporations. A pack of lies! In fact, *our ideological ancestors were champions of the poor, the powerless and the weak.* They were champions of persecuted racial, ethnic, cultural and religious minorities as well as the foremost advocates for the rights of the accused and prisoners. The Liberty Movement has much work to do to repair its false image.

Summary. Liberalism was a beautiful set of interlocking ideas that helped liberate humanity from age-old poverty, oppression and despair from 1650 through 1900. Though the liberal era ended, many of its ideas and accomplishments continue and are responsible for most of what is good about the modern world.

Liberalism remains a viable threat to replace progressivism as the prevailing political ideology. Unlike conservatism, liberalism is a coherent ideology with a positive program that not only has worked in practice but is largely responsible for making America great in the first place. Liberalism built the country. Progressivism has nearly destroyed it. Progressivism has been a disastrous historical experiment that failed. It is time to restore liberalism as our political ideal. In the past, liberalism suffered because its program of liberating humanity from the state and the old regime was never fully executed, understood and supported and liberals were blamed for the negative effects of policies they opposed. This time, as Rothbard has advised, we must not repeat the mistake of applying liberalism piecemeal while retaining aspects of the evil old regime.

Liberalism rising from the dead to defeat progressivism as it had previously defeated prior forms of state tyranny would be a stupendous historical achievement. The ancient scourge of mankind is the threat and reality of organized violence. In very few times and places, mostly when living in isolation or in very small groups, have human beings known that rare joy that comes from knowing that when you wake up in the morning, you may do as you please with what you own. *Liberalism was, in effect, a concerted effort by great and courageous minds to stamp out violence in human affairs, especially state violence.* Liberalism was in the midst of this momentous work, deconstructing the various rationales for state power and constructing the doctrines of natural rights and spontaneous market order. However, before liberalism's work was done but after enormous progress had been made, progressivism intervened, defeated liberalism politically (not intellectually), and created a positive theory of state violence that was far more compelling than all the prior and competing versions.

What explains the remarkable success of progressivism in rescuing the notion of aggressive state violence from virtual defeat by liberalism and making it stronger than ever? Human beings universally oppose aggressive violence in its palpable form. That's why there is no political party that takes the side of murder, slavery, rape, and armed robbery. The old regime, unconcerned with the niceties of due process and other humanitarian values propounded by liberalism, was brutal. Taxes were collected at sword point, soldiers conscripted by brute force, criminal suspects locked up in dungeons and forgotten. It did not take a monumental mental effort to grasp its evil nature. Similarly, the evil of the various totalitarianism regimes, Nazi Germany, Stalinist Russia and Pol Pot's Cambodia, was apparent.

Progressivism, however, was superimposed upon liberalism, which, by overthrowing the old regime and installing relatively benign governments, engendered an attitude of compliance with law and a sense of the legitimacy of the government. Liberal regimes also used voting and majority rule as mechanisms to staff their governments if not to determine the limits of power which were set instead by fundamental principles and by written constitutions. *Thus, liberalism, by legitimizing the state and voting and majority rule, sowed the seeds of its own demise by validating mechanisms whose scope and significance progressives would greatly expand.*

Along the same lines, in sharp contrast to kingdoms and dictatorships, in democracies, the people tend to identify with the government. Under liberalism, much of what government did was defensive in nature. Thus, it was unusual and counterintuitive in that era to view government as a violent institution as the bulk of its force was used *defensively* and approved democratically. When, under progressivism, government began to use ever more *aggressive* force and violence, it remained for many decades protected by its former image of benevolence.

Further, pragmatic progressives deny the existence of objective truth such as the intrinsic wrongfulness of violence and they judge truth not by the nature of the action but by its consequences. When in the bleak years of liberalism, its champions would call the state a band of criminals, the progressive mind would presumably think, that's merely your opinion and even if it's true, I like their programs and their consequences. At all times in the process, progressives could rely on the support of the vast majority of intellectuals, writers, teachers and artists to convince the public, in Swiftian terms, that black is white or white is black "according as they are paid."[162]

The propaganda campaign to hide from the public the fact that government uses violence in all it does has been immensely aided by the fact that its use of force is *latent* 99.99% of the time. Most people do not want to confront the state and its *gendarmes* and thus only rarely does the state feel the need to use blatant force such as at Wounded Knee, Kent State, Waco and Ruby Ridge and expose its true nature. Only true liberals seem to know the truth: if you resist the state's edicts and exercise your natural right to *defend* your life, liberty and property from the state, you will be shot to death.

Because of the successful efforts of progressives to somehow convince the vast majority of Americans to believe obvious absurdities: that the state is not an inherently aggressive institution or that it has every moral right to use aggressive force, mankind is once again suffering from its age-old political pestilence: the constant threat of being beaten to a pulp by a group stronger than you merely for exercising your natural right to do what you wish with what you own.

What a tragedy!

---

[162] *Gulliver's Travels.*

6. Progressivism's Vanquished Foe— Conservatism

After Progressivism replaced liberalism as America's dominant ideology, liberals faded from the scene and, like the cheetah, almost went extinct. From 1900 through 1960, as the saying goes, all the prominent liberals in America could have fit into Murray Rothbard's living room.

Nature abhors a vacuum so conservatism stepped into the void left by the apparent death of liberalism. Sandwiched in between progressive Republicans Taft and Hoover were two men who could be considered conservatives in the contemporary sense: Harding and Coolidge. Harding did cut spending and Coolidge kept spending low in his brief tenure; however, neither rolled back the basic progressive tools of the modern welfare-warfare state, the income tax and the Federal Reserve. They created no movement and had little if any lasting influence over American politics. The next several GOP nominees and Presidents can safely be classified as progressives: Hoover, Alf Landon, Wendell Willkie, Thomas E. Dewey, Eisenhower and Nixon.

Modern conservatism as a political force dates from 1964 when Barry Goldwater won the Republican nomination for President. Goldwater's losing but energetic campaign paved the way for the rise of Ronald Reagan in 1980. Thus, from 1964 through 1980, conservatism was the dominant force within the GOP and had the full attention of the American people. In 1980, conservatives took power, capturing the White House and the Senate. That began an era during which conservatives held actual political power in at least one branch of the federal government for 27 out of 33 years. Overall, we can calculate that conservatives have held center stage in American politics for fifty years. Conservatives cannot complain that they never had a chance to make their case and never had control over the levers of power.

Let's examine the conservative era more closely. During this era, conservatives held the White House for at least sixteen years—Reagan, 1981-1988; Bush I, 1989-1992; Bush II, 2001-2008. I will concede that calling Bush I a conservative is a stretch but he at least had to pander to the conservative base of his party.

The Republicans held the Senate from 1981-1986; 1995-2000; part of 2001; and 2003-2006. The Republicans took the House in 1994 in a "revolution" that had conservative and libertarian elements. While they restrained spending with a hostile Bill Clinton in the White House, they accomplished little to roll back big government. They controlled the House until 2006 and then from 2011 to the present.

Ronald Reagan appointed four justices to the Supreme Court. Bush I appointed two and Bush II added two more. The Court is now considered to have a 5-4 moderate conservative majority.

With all this raw political power, has conservatism been able to roll back the progressive state? Quite the contrary. *The federal government is bigger and stronger than ever.*

Under Reagan, federal spending increased faster than it did under Clinton and Obama![163] LBJ's Medicare program was expanded. The Veterans Administration was made a cabinet department and over 200,000 civilian employees were added to the payroll.[164] The war on drugs, a classic progressive idea, was escalated and the drug czar's office was created. Reagan "saved" another classic progressive program, Social Security, by increasing the payroll tax. Debt and inflation increased. Instead of cutting spending, Reagan raised taxes six times to pay for the insolvent progressive state built up by Wilson, FDR and Johnson. The moderate conservative Bush I signed the Americans with Disabilities Act, an open-ended invitation for continual government growth in that area.

---

[163] D. Mitchell, "Mirror, Mirror, on the Wall, Which President Is the Biggest Spender of All?" *Forbes.com*, May 24, 2012 (counting all spending and adjusted for inflation).

[164] S. Richman, "The Sad Legacy of Ronald Reagan," *The Free Market* (Oct. 1988).

Progressivism's Vanquished Foe—Conservatism

The "revolutionary" 1994 GOP Congress increased federal spending and taxes collected each year. They eviscerated the ancient right of Englishmen and Americans—*habeas corpus*. They flunked the acid test of economic sanity—raising the minimum wage (mandatory unemployment law). They also passed the Freedom to Farm Act (at taxpayers' expense, that is). Spending was relatively restrained in the mid-to-late 1990's but that can be explained by the extremely hostile relationship with Bill Clinton.

The worst performance came under Bush II. Under Bush, the GOP briefly held both branches of Congress and also had a sympathetic Supreme Court for the most part. Spending increased under Bush II and he added a gigantic new welfare program, the so-called prescription drug benefit. Bush II appointed Chief Judge Roberts who would later cast the deciding vote for Obamacare, one of the biggest progressive programs in the last 100 years.

Why did conservatism fail in its duel with the progressive state? First, conservatism is an incoherent and ill-defined doctrine. It is difficult to defeat a powerful and appealing set of ideas like progressivism with such a vague doctrine. Who will go to the barricades for a mishmash? Few, apparently. Progressivism offers a simple and very satisfying panacea for all human ills. Conservatism offers hostility to that simple solution without offering up an alternative vision.

Second, American conservatism is a reaction to progressivism as opposed to a positive doctrine itself. It defines itself as an attempt to slow down progressivism. As Mises argued, "conservatism is an empty program. It is merely negative, rejecting any change." Mises also asked rhetorically, what do conservatives stand for?[165] In the battle for public opinion between progressivism, which promises utopia on earth via the government and cost-free as well, and conservatives who said either "No" or "slow down," it is no surprise that progressivism has defeated conservatism for decades and especially currently. Similarly, Hayek argued correctly that conservatism:

---

[165] Jorg Guido Hulsmann, *Mises: The Last Knight of Liberalism*, Mises Institute, Auburn (2007), p. 922.

> "by its very nature . . . cannot offer an alternative to the direction in which we are moving. It may succeed by its resistance to current tendencies in slowing down undesirable developments, but, since it does not indicate another direction, it cannot prevent their continuance. *It has, for this reason, invariably been the fate of conservatism to be dragged along a path not of its own choosing.* The tug of war between conservatives and progressives can only affect the speed, not the direction, of contemporary developments."[166]

Hayek identified other critical flaws of conservatism as an antagonist to progressivism. Conservatives, he argues, are too willing to use government force to preserve authority and to impose moral values on others: "like the socialist, [the conservative] regards himself as entitled to force the values he holds on other people." This explains for example why conservatives have willingly signed onto the "war on drugs" started by the progressives. Hayek also notes that conservatives tend to be nationalists (entitled to place their nation's interests over others), thus inclining them to statist policies such as protectionism and imperialism and war.[167] Hayek aptly calls nationalism "the bridge from conservatism to collectivism." Mises agrees:

> "Economic nationalism, the necessary complement of domestic interventionism, hurts the interests of foreign peoples and thus creates international conflict. It suggests the idea of amending this unsatisfactory state of affairs by war. . . . Interventionism generates economic nationalism, and economic nationalism generates bellicosity. If men and commodities are prevented from crossing the borderlines, why should not the armies try to pave the way for them? . . .

---

[166] "Why I Am Not a Conservative," in *The Constitution of Liberty* (Chicago: The University of Chicago Press, 1960), p. 520 (emphasis added).

[167] *Id.*

> Modern civilization is a product of the philosophy of laissez faire. It cannot be preserved under the ideology of government omnipotence. . . . The main thing is to discard the ideology that generates war. [p. 831-2]"[168]

Third, as argued in Chapter 2, we are all progressives now. Conservative and Republican politicians instinctively know this and therefore, even if they were so inclined, moving against the progressive state would be to risk their power and position. Power and position are seductive things when weighed against a fuzzy ideology lacking a positive vision.

Fourth, however conservatism is defined, liberty is not its highest priority so in that sense it shares the basic premise of progressivism that government force, in some cases, can produce a better result than free individuals voluntarily cooperating in society. The conservative thus faces the difficult task of explaining why government intervention is useless here but not there. In practice, logrolling occurs. To preserve the coercive aspect of their agenda, they have traded away the libertarian element to progressives in deals that enhanced whatever it is that the progressives wanted at that time. For example, conservatives signed onto the welfare state lest they lose the power they needed to coerce morality and fight their global crusade against communism and terrorism. Progressives, fearful of being seen as soft on communism, lose power and be unable to create the "Great Society," decided to fight the communists in Vietnam. The reason Bush I reneged on his "no new taxes" pledge was to gain progressive support for the Gulf War. Bush II allowed domestic spending to rise as he was busy garnering support for his Asian land wars.

What was useful in conservatism's battle with progressivism was the small and watered-down element of fiscal conservatism. However, this presumptive support for liberty in fiscal matters was countervailed by a disregard of liberty in foreign policy and matters of personal freedom.

---

[168] *Human Action: A Treatise on Economics* (Contemporary Books: Chicago, 3rd. Rev. ed., 1949) p. 831.

Progressivism's Vanquished Foe—Conservatism

As the above examples illustrate, superficial differences between and among various ideologies on the basis of the kinds of government intervention they favor, are essentially illusory. All government intervention — foreign, military, cultural, or economic — involves the use of force to transfer life, liberty or property from some people to others, causing negative consequences for the victimized group, and leading to demands for further intervention to remedy the problems caused by the initial intervention. Support for intervention in one area, by reinforcing the principle that force is an efficacious means of solving human problems, tends to legitimize intervention in other policy areas. Since progressives and conservatives believe in the use of aggressive force *in principle*, they lack a principled basis for opposing its use even in ways that make them uncomfortable.

Since *power* is their ultimate premise, conservatives will logroll over liberty to maintain their power. In the end, we got all the bad stuff even though certain groups paid lip service against each program: Cold War, hot war, war on poverty, drug war. Notice that all these wars were brought to you by a coalition government of progressives and conservatives and featured massive centralized state coercion aimed at preventing Americans from living their lives as they wished. You cannot trust conservatives to advance liberty. In the end, they will choose power over principle and power over you.

Regardless of how they describe themselves, or for what particular reasons they wish to push people around, progressives *and conservatives* can be counted on to join forces to oppose the dangerous concept that individuals have the right to control their own bodies, minds, and property.

Finally, conservatives have a progressive-like faith in the efficacy of government when it comes to the military, police and war. This causes two problems. Progressives have frequently drawn an analogy between government at war and domestic policy in order to re-create its awesome and centralized power on the home front. Conservatives are powerless to disagree. More importantly, war and foreign intervention have negative consequences on the home front which create demands for increased government intervention. Government creates its own demand.

Examples abound. The Civil War disabled many men and created many widows and orphans, leading to a demand for veterans' pensions. These pensions created a demand for broader coverage leading ultimately to Social Security. World War II disrupted the lives of millions of men leading to a demand for educational aid under the G. I. Bill. This created the model and the demand for a broader program—student loans. Veterans' hospitals created the model for socialized medicine. Many of the advocates of the Great Society had fought in World War II and wanted to use the war model to create a War on Poverty. Similarly, many New Dealers had their first experience in central economic planning under World War I and put that experience to work under FDR.[169] War is truly the health of the state domestically as well.

The failure of constitutionalism. Conservatism is a reaction to progressivism and its essence is to be *against progressivism* as opposed to having a positive program. To fill the void, conservatives have often repaired to the safe harbor of *constitutionalism* as a substitute for a coherent ideology. There are numerous problems with constitutionalism as a bulwark against progressivism and constitutionalism has been and will continue to be a spectacular failure in staunching the continual growth of progressive government.

First and foremost, there is no way to enforce the Constitution against the government as the government itself claims the right to interpret and enforce the document in any dispute with a private citizen. For example, in the "Pork Lawsuit,"[170] I represented fifty solid citizens who sought to finally enforce New York State's 160 year-old ban on the state giving money to private business firms. The language of the provision was crystal clear: "The money of the state shall not be given or loaned to or in aid of any private corporation or association, or private undertaking. . ."[171] In spite of this clear language, the state was routinely giving out *billions* of dollars in outright cash grants to private firms. Much to my cynic's surprise, we won 5-0 in the

---

[169] See, M. Rothbard, "Left and Right: The Prospects for Liberty," in *Egalitarianism: A Revolt Against Nature and Other Essays*, p. 36.

[170] *Bordeleau v. New York State*, 18 N.Y.3d 305 (2011).

[171] NY Const. Article VII, § 8 (1).

Appellate Division, the State's second highest court. Having zero faith in government courts, I threw out the winning brief in that Court and started from scratch, producing a much stronger case for our side. At oral argument, which you can watch on You Tube,[172] the State's attorney gave a long, rambling and incoherent speech and was unable to cogently answer questions from the judges.

Nevertheless, in spite of the clear language on our side, not to mention the unambiguous legislative history and all reasonable policy arguments, we lost 5-2 in the Court of Appeals in an opinion by a judge who was as silent as the Sphinx at oral argument. There were two blistering dissents by Judge Eugene Pigott and by Judge Robert Smith (reputed to be a libertarian!), who all but accused the majority of treason ("judicially repealing" the Constitution).

Now, what do you do when the government judicially erases the Constitution? You can either grin and bear it, which is what we did, or you can muster a million-man army, go to Albany, depose the Court, replace it with a court with better reading comprehension skills, and stop corporate handouts. Here's the problem: you will probably be arrested by the FBI as soon as you announce your intentions. Second, even if you could secret a million-man army into downtown Albany, the PSA would simply muster a three million man army and defeat you on the battlefield in a day or two, with the ninety percent of the public that is progressive, cheering wildly as you are slaughtered in the streets or rounded up and put into a government cage[173] for fifty years. So, again, the problem, *a fatal one*, with constitutions is that there is no way to enforce them short of war. Yet, surely the argument for a constitution in the first place is to resolve disputes over the limits of government power *without going to war!* Thus, constitutionalism failed.

The Constitution is *not* a contract, however, since many view it as such, it will be useful to assume for the sake of argument that it is a contract. Would you sign a contract with a private firm that gave that firm sole power to interpret and enforce the contract? Would you sign a contract with a roofer that, in effect, allowed him to charge you $15,000 and not put a roof on your house? Only a fool would do so,

---

[172] https://www.youtube.com/watch?v=UVSjrZrUWRU
[173] A term popularized by Lew Rockwell.

yet, the Constitution is precisely such a sham "contract" as it gives the other party to it sole power to adjudicate any disputes about it. It is yet another nail in the coffin of conservatism that its chief ideological bulwark, constitutionalism, turns out to be a sophisticated hoax!

As if the above flaws were not enough, constitutionalism has other problems insofar as it purports to be a bulwark against progressivism. Surely, many constitutionalists believe that the constitution is a statement of various underlying *objective truths* about the world, human nature, government and politics. This overlooks the fact that progressives are pragmatists, that is, folks who reject the notion that there is an objective reality outside our minds that we can know and express in words understandable to other people. To cite a constitution to a progressive is like speaking Mandarin to a Martian or English to a wall. It's a pointless exercise since pragmatists reject the notion of objective truth and are solely interested in the practical consequences of ideas and words. Thus, in the Pork Lawsuit, the five progressive judges in the majority, *including two conservative Republicans,* no doubt believed that state government must have the tools of economic development to compete with other states and countries that have them. They were oblivious to whether the Constitution of 1846 was *true or not.* It was, in 2011, no longer practical. The bottom line is that the 90 percent of the public that is progressive, elected progressive governors who appointed progressive judges who gave us a progressive result, the Constitution be damned!

Yet another fatal flaw with the United States Constitution is that, while its Bill of Rights was libertarian in nature and origin, the actual body of the Constitution created the framework for an extremely powerful federal government. Proof of this fact is Robert "Brutus" Yates' essay, Antifederalist No. 1, wherein he demonstrates through ineluctable logic how a huge and powerful federal government could and likely would evolve from the extensive powers granted to the three branches of government in that document. He was right as it turns out:

> "It is true this government is limited to certain objects,
> or to speak more properly, some small degree of power
> is still left to the states, but a little attention to the

powers vested in the general government, will convince every candid man, that if it is capable of being executed, all that is reserved for the individual states must very soon be annihilated, except so far as they are barely necessary to the organization of the general government. The powers of the general legislature extend to every case that is of the least importance — there is nothing valuable to human nature, nothing dear to freemen, but what is within its power. It has authority to make laws which will affect the lives, the liberty, and property of every man in the United States; nor can the constitution or laws of any state, in any way prevent or impede the full and complete execution of every power given. The legislative power is competent to lay taxes, duties, imposts, and excises; — *there is no limitation to this power*, unless it be said that the clause which directs the use to which those taxes, and duties shall be applied, may be said to be a limitation: but this is no restriction of the power at all, for by this clause they are to be applied to pay the debts and provide for the common defence and general welfare of the United States; but the legislature have authority to contract debts at their discretion; they are the sole judges of what is necessary to provide for the common defence, and they only are to determine what is for the general welfare; *this power therefore is neither more nor less, than a power to lay and collect taxes, imposts, and excises, at their pleasure; not only [is] the power to lay taxes unlimited, as to the amount they may require, but it is perfect and absolute to raise them in any mode they please.* No state legislature, or any power in the state governments, have any more to do in carrying this into effect, than the authority of one state has to do with that of another. *In the business therefore of laying and collecting taxes, the idea of confederation is totally lost, and that of one entire republic is embraced.* It is proper here to remark, that the authority to lay and collect taxes is the most important of any power that can be granted; it connects with it almost all other powers, or at least will in process of time draw all other after it; it is the great means of protection, security, and defence, in a good government, and the great engine of oppression and tyranny in a bad one. This cannot fail of being the case, if we consider the contracted limits which are set by this constitution, to the late [state?] governments, on this article of raising money. No state can emit paper money — lay any duties, or imposts, on imports, or exports, but by consent of the Congress; and then the net produce shall be for the benefit of the United States: the only means therefore left, for any state to support its government and discharge its debts, is by direct taxation; and the United States have also power to lay and collect taxes, in any way they please. Every one who has thought on the subject, must be convinced that but small sums of money can be collected in any country, by direct taxe[s], when the foederal government begins to exercise the right of taxation in all its parts, the legislatures of the several states will find it impossible to raise monies to support their governments. Without money they cannot be supported, and they must dwindle away, and, as before observed, their powers absorbed in that of the general government." (Emphasis added.)

So, in the battle against progressivism, constitutionalism is worse than useless as it cannot accomplish the goal and will simply distract us and mollify us into drilling an infinite number of dry holes. The rejection of constitutionalism as a strategy is yet another reason for us to disassociate from the conservative movement.

GOP Politics in a Nutshell. The utter failure of conservative Republicans to combat progressivism in any meaningful way explains the nature of GOP politics today. Like the Seinfeld sitcom, it is much ado about nothing, but without the laughs.

Having failed to roll back any major progressive program in the last *100 years*, how does the GOP manage to keep the votes and donations of the rank and file flowing in in sufficient quantities to keep the GOP machine in power? Highly paid and talented GOP consultants have brilliantly risen to the challenge. There must be something that keeps the troops anteing up their votes and legwork and contributions to the mendacious Republican machine that talks smaller government but *never* delivers. There is. Here is how the scam works. The GOP whips up a personal hatred of prominent Democrats as a red herring to distract their own rank and file away from their lengthy record of failure.

How do members of the GOP machine—elected and party officials, government employees and contractors, lawyers, consultants, and lobbyists, keep the gravy train rolling? Not by proposing to roll back the very same progressive big government that the rank and file basically supports. That would likely involve losing elections which would threaten to cut off the money spigot. Rather, the GOP machine deliberately distracts the rank and file's attention away from ideas, issues and policies, and manipulates the masses into personally hating the leading Democrats *du jour*. Brilliant! Well done. These operatives, by the way, think that Ron Paul and any other activists who really care about ideas are saps and they are laughing at us all the way to the bank.

Hillary was right. There *is* a vast, right-wing conspiracy to whip up hatred of Democratic icons like Bill and Hillary and Barack and Michelle primarily for their personal peccadilloes. So long as you hate Obama personally, you won't be focusing on the GOP's pathetic record of never shrinking government. Who cares if the GOP-controlled House continues to vote to fund progressive big government? What's really important is that rascal Obama golfs too much and Michelle takes too many vacations. The nerve!

Conclusion. Conservatism is an idea whose time has come and gone. While historical liberalism has a long list of monumental accomplishments, one struggles to conjure up a single significant accomplishment of American conservatism. Conservatism will never wage a winning war against progressivism. Worse yet, because of its half-hearted defense of market economics; its glorification of militarism and war and law enforcement; its often hostile attitude towards civil liberties; and its endless compromises with progressives to maintain power, the Liberty Movement's various dalliances with this failed ideology have produced nothing of value, have tainted the Movement and have caused confusion about its true nature. *The Liberty Movement must sever its ties to conservatism and move forward.*

7.   War is the Health of the Progressive State

Progressivism is inherently violent and aggressive. It is, after all, a theory of the beneficence of state violence. It should be no surprise then that progressivism and progressives have been behind and in front of many of the great and small wars of our times. However, since the vast majority of Americans are progressives, this *fact* will undoubtedly come as a big and unpleasant surprise. So be it.

Calling the Civil War "progressive" will surprise many people. After all, the Progressive Era had not even begun yet. The subject of this book, however, is the idea or cluster of ideas that is progressivism, not the particular manifestation of those ideas that we call the Progressive Era. Nevertheless, capital "P" Progressive Theodore Roosevelt, quoted in Chapter 3, called Lincoln a "radical progressive."

There is much confusion about the cause or causes of the Civil War. The prevailing view is that the war was "about" slavery or the cause of the war was slavery. The argument then proceeds to note that one reason or the main reason why the South seceded was to preserve slavery. However, secession was not the cause of the war! It's not surprising there is so much confusion on this point as the concept of causation is not well understood or defined. I suggest that the cause of an event is the sum total of all factors that must combine at a certain time and place to produce the event. Clearly, if the Union had let the South secede, there would have been no war. The war, therefore, was *caused by* the Union's response which was to send a huge army into Virginia to forcibly bring the states back into a union they had joined voluntarily. This was the proximate cause of the war. Why did the Union invade the South? Lincoln was clear on this point: to preserve the union. Why?

War is the Health of the Progressive State

Progressivism is inherently a centralizing movement. Progressivism favors the use of government force to improve society. The purpose of force is to negate the mind and will of the victims so they no longer make their own choices with respect to the subject matter of the force. *When force is applied to human relations, power is centralized.* Liberty allows power to be decentralized and dispersed to individuals. *Force centralizes power.* When a bank robber points a gun at the teller, he is centralizing power to himself. "For what are robberies themselves, but little kingdoms."[174]

If force is good for society, then it follows that the greater number of people subjected to that force, the better. States, regions and provinces exempt from a particular use of force are deprived of the "benefits" of that force and therefore *the progressive is always working towards expanding the geographic scope of his policies.* By the same logic, the progressive instinctively opposes secession, which reduces the scope of his coercive policies. *Thus, Lincoln's desire to preserve the union by brutal violence if necessary was a quintessentially progressive act.*

Even if the Confederacy had freed the slaves, the Union would still have invaded, conquered and ruled the South! In fact, the South did in fact free the slaves in 1865 and yet, *149 years later,* the Federales still occupy the South and dominate and exploit Southerners, both black and white. Indeed, the historical myth that the Civil War was fought to improve the welfare of the slaves is called into question by this undeniable fact: Southern blacks were less free after the war than Southern whites were before it. The true purpose of the war was to make the central government more powerful and it succeeded brilliantly.

It should be noted that wherever one finds turbulence and war around the globe *today*, the cause is usually the same: strangers in distant capitals dictating to others they do not know, who live, far, far away, how they shall live. The victims naturally resist the imperialists with all the force they can muster. Don't blame the victims as the progressive American media and political elite invariably do in such cases.

---

[174] St. Augustine. See, R. McMaken, Peace and State Coercion in Augustine's Thought, *LewRockwell.com*, Oct. 2, 2014.

War is the Health of the Progressive State

Domestic political goals. A myriad of domestic political concerns have led democracies into war. Modern democracies tend to extensively intervene in the free market by means of high taxes, welfare, and subsidies in order to buy the votes that keep the politicians in power. As Ludwig von Mises demonstrated, each intervention into the economy causes problems that lead to the demand for ever further interventions. Government thereby creates its own demand. Eventually, the economic problems become intractable, leading to the inevitable temptation to create a foreign policy distraction.[175] Combine that with the fact that war, while undeniably harming the economy, gives the appearance of stimulating the economy, and we have a formula for why progressive governments would have a motive for war.

For example, the Great Depression was caused by the Federal Reserve's expansion of the money supply in the late 1920's.[176] Franklin Roosevelt's New Deal had failed to bring America out of the Great Depression as late as 1941. Many believe that FDR welcomed American entrance into World War II to distract attention from his domestic policy failures or in the hope that the war would get the economy moving again. Such theories cannot definitively be proven. What cannot be denied is that FDR did everything he possibly could do to goad either Germany or Japan into attacking the United States.

Why did the United States fight a pointless war in Vietnam? One theory is that President Kennedy escalated U.S. involvement because he had accused President Eisenhower in 1960 of being "soft" on communism. When Lyndon Johnson came to power, he had ambitious domestic plans for creating a "Great Society," and could not afford to lose political capital over the "loss" of another country to communism.[177]

---

[175] See, Walter Karp, *The Politics of War* (New York: Harper Colophon, 1979).

[176] Murray Rothbard, *America's Great Depression* (1963).

[177] R. Raico, *supra* at 73.

War is the Health of the Progressive State

Progressives have also supported war as a means to introduce their command and control economies. Historian Ralph Raico quotes John Dewey's enthusiasm about World War I:

> "In every warring country there has been the same demand that in the time of great national stress production for profit be subordinated to production for use. Legal possession and individual property rights have had to give way before social requirements. The old conception of the absoluteness of property the world over has received a blow from which it will never wholly recover. Conscription has brought home to countries which have been the home of the individualistic tradition the supremacy of public need over private possession. No matter how many among the special agencies for public control decay with the disappearance of the war stress, the movement will never go backward."[178]

Special interest politics. Special interest group politics is a flaw of progressivism. By focusing their efforts, votes, and campaign contributions, small segments of the population can exercise influence on policy all out of proportion to their numbers. This is frequently seen in domestic policy. For example, the sugar lobby is responsible for the sugar quota which limits the amount of foreign sugar that can be imported into the United States. The result is billions of dollars in sales that benefit a few companies and their employees. Every other person in the country suffers. Because the people who gain, gain much, they are moved to lobby for this law. The people who lose, lose only a little, and thus do nothing to repeal the law.

Democracies feature all kinds of absurd laws and policies that benefit a few at the expense of everyone else. What is rarely remarked,

---

[178] "America's Foreign Policy—The Turning Point, 1998-1919, in *The Failure of America' Foreign Wars*, Richard M. Ebeling and Jacob G. Hornberger, ed., Future of Freedom Foundation, 1996, pp. 73.

however, is that this special interest group analysis applies to foreign policy as well. For example, there are over 150 million Arabs in the Middle East, mostly Muslims, and they have over one billion coreligionists around the world. Arab countries have vast oil reserves. Yet, for over sixty years, United States foreign policy has favored the tiny state of Israel, much to the chagrin of these Arab and Islamic millions. This is a foreign policy most decidedly *not* in the interests of the average American. This policy has dragged the United States into every aspect of the ongoing conflict over the Middle East. In addition to supplying massive military aid to Israel, American troops have shed blood nearby in Lebanon in a related conflict. Further, there is reason to believe that the terrorist attacks on September 11th were in part in retaliation for American support for Israel. As a result of those attacks, the United States is in the midst of an endless Asian land war in Afghanistan.

There are other examples of countries getting into wars to advance discrete private agendas. Ralph Raico writes that most Americans wanted the United States to stay out of World War I, except for the East Coast economic and social elite which had close business and social ties to England.[179] The United States has engaged in numerous military actions at the behest of private corporations that were foolish enough to invest in countries where property rights were insecure. The United States fought a major war in Kuwait and Iraq the only apparent reason for which was to preserve an oriental despotism. Surely, the actual reason was to protect certain discrete private interests in oil in Kuwait and Saudi Arabia. From any practical point of view, the dispute did not concern the average American in the slightest. They would buy their gasoline as usual at the pump, at prices set by the vagaries of the world oil market, regardless of which crooked Middle East sheikh sold the rights to oil (he had previously stolen) to some private company. Thus, once again war was fought by a progressive democracy to advance a special interest.

Messianic goals. Democracies are vulnerable to messianic crusades. Progressive politicians have a sense of moral superiority which impels them to reform other nations just as they seek to reform their own

---

[179] *Id.* at pp. 66-67.

citizens and societies. Woodrow Wilson is the foremost example of this spirit: "America is henceforth to stand for the assertion of the right of one nation to serve the other nations of the world."[40] The temptation to add, ". . . whether they like it or not," is irresistible. Thus, the messianic impulse (rationalization?) would launch America into the disastrous World War I, and later wars such as Vietnam, the Gulf War, and the bombing of Serbia.

Imperialism. Oftentimes, democracies end up in wars that were seemingly started by non-democracies. For example, the United States presumably got involved in World War II because of the Japanese attack on Pearl Harbor. The reality is more complex. What was in dispute was which nation would be the dominant power in East Asia. America had staked its imperial claim forty-three years earlier by going to war with Spain. Subsequently, in a bloody war, Progressive America seized the Philippines from the natives. Japan invaded China in 1937. America applied diplomatic and economic pressure on Japan and demanded that Japan leave China. An oil embargo was imposed. Japan responded by seizing the oil fields of Malaysia and, anticipating American opposition, struck Pearl Harbor. The genesis of the conflict, however, was America's (democratic) imperial designs on East Asia.[180]

Democracies also have the means to fight wars. Analysts of war spend much time thinking about *why* wars are fought and far too little time contemplating the *means* of war. The resources for war are acquired by *conscription, taxation, confiscation, and inflation.* Without cannon and cannon fodder, there are no wars. In modern times, politicians neither fight nor pay for the wars they start or join. With their aura of legitimacy, democracies are particularly adept at utilizing all these

---

[180] See generally, R. Ebeling, "Covering the Map of the world: The Half Century Legacy of the Yalta Conference, in The Failure of America' Foreign Wars, Richard M. Ebeling and Jacob G. Hornberger, ed., Future of Freedom Foundation, 1996, pp. 160, 178-180; Thomas E. Woods, *The Politically Incorrect Guide to American History* Regnery Publishing Inc., Washington, D.C. 2004), pp. 179-181; J. Denson, "Franklin Delano Roosevelt and the First Shot: A study of Deceit and Deception," in Reassessing the Presidency: The Rise of the Executive State and the Decline of Freedom, Mises Institute, 2001.

means. Since citizens tend to identify with the democratic state, there is usually little trouble conscripting troops and confiscating the economic resources required for war.[181] Perhaps this is why democracies tend to win the wars they fight. War is the health of the state, but the democratic state is also the health of war.

In contrast to progressive democracies, liberal republics such as the one the progressives replaced around 1900, discourage war. Republics differ from democracies in that they rely on militias, not conscription, for defense. The militia system is a powerful deterrent to invasion. To achieve victory, an invading army, with long supply lines, must subdue the entire able-bodied population, fighting in their own backyards. As the Civil War demonstrated, it is a mistake for the invaded state to gather up its men into standing armies, and then go confront the invading army in set-piece battles in which the defenders are outnumbered. Militia and guerilla tactics would probably have carried the day. Conversely, militias are poor offensive weapons. They therefore discourage aggressive or imperialistic wars. They also thereby discourage preemptive strikes by other states that would otherwise fear invasion. Financially, republics have little or no taxation with which to fund aggressive war. Aggressive war lies beyond their constitutional mandate and the pursuit of such a war is likely to be resisted internally by well-armed citizens. *Pure republics are unlikely to start wars, or lose them.*

The imperial impulse springs mainly from the power elite. Ordinary people are less interested in conquering far-off places. The problem is, members of modern power elites are rarely interested in doing any actual fighting. Nor can a republican militia do the fighting. Thus, the elites turned inevitably to conscription, a concept alien to a free society. A brief survey of the history of American conscription shows its close link to imperial aims. Conscription was first proposed in the War of 1812 to provide troops to *invade* Canada. It was defeated in Congress. Conscription, opposed by New England in 1812, was supported by New England in 1863 to provide the Union with troops to *invade* the South. Citizens were conscripted to fight *in Europe* in

---

[181] See, M. Rothbard, "Anatomy of the State," in *Egalitarianism As a Revolt Against Nature and Other Essays*. Washington, DC: Libertarian Review Press, 1974.

War is the Health of the Progressive State

1917—1918. Troops were conscripted to fight *in Europe and Asia* in 1941—45. Troops were conscripted to fight *in Korea and Vietnam*. Conscription must be seen as an important tool of imperialism and war.

Summary. The history and evidence of America's bellicosity in the progressive era is thoroughly explained by a theoretical examination of democracies' motives for war and means to wage them. Progressive democracies tend to be aggressive, imperialistic, and warlike. These tendencies provoke terrorism—the weapon of the weak—which in turn provokes further foreign intervention, and more terrorism, in an endless cycle of violence. While they tend to be aggressive abroad, they continually grow domestically, in power, scope and size. They ever-increase the property and liberty they confiscate. They stir up ethnic and religious hostilities by pushing towards one way of life for all groups, whether the politically weaker groups like it or not.

Though, in theory, a democracy could choose to be quite libertarian, establishing a minimal state limited to protecting individual rights and private property, this is a faint hope. The more realistic view is that there is an inherent and unavoidable tension between individual rights and democracy. If individuals are to be allowed to own themselves and do what they wish with their justly acquired property, what exactly is the role of the "will of the people" or the majority or the legislature? Either these democratic mechanisms will rubber stamp those rights, in which case, these mechanisms are superfluous, or, they will overrule those rights, in which case democracy becomes the enemy of libertarian rights and therefore, an enemy of peace.

Two of the most important wars in modern history were fought in part for the express purpose of advancing democratic principles. In the case of World War I, this is well known. Woodrow Wilson called it the war "to make the world safe for democracy." We have heard this refrain over and over again as the rationalization for war: in Korea, Vietnam, and the Balkans. As previously discussed, Lincoln explicitly justified the bloody Civil War as a war to save majority rule.

The modus operandi of progressive democracy is closer to that of dictatorships than is commonly thought. Though these regimes differ in the manner that leaders are selected, they differ little in the manner in which they relate to their individual subjects on a daily basis: *both*

144

regimes impose their will by force! True, most democracies have in storage pieces of paper with words printed on them (constitutions) which supposedly limit the amount of force they can use. Alas, as Orwell taught us, words can mean virtually whatever we want them to mean.[46] At the end of the day, the progressive democratic state has the most powerful dictionary: the army.

As Hans-Hermann Hoppe explains, United States intervention into World War I, *to advance democracy*, was the great catastrophe of the 20[th]century:

> "If the United States had followed a strict non-interventionist foreign policy, it is likely that the intra-European conflict would have ended in late 1916 or early 1917 as the result of several peace initiatives, most notably by the Austrian Emperor Charles I. Moreover, the war would have been concluded with a mutually acceptable and face-saving compromise peace rather than the actual dictate. Consequently, Austria-Hungary, Germany and Russia would have remained traditional monarchies instead of being turned into short-lived democratic republics. With a Russian Czar and a German and Austrian Kaiser in place, it would have been almost impossible for the Bolsheviks to seize power in Russia, and in reaction to a growing communist threat in Western Europe, for the Fascists and National Socialists to do the same in Italy and Germany. Millions of victims of communism, national socialism, and World War II would have been saved. The extent of government interference with and control of the private economy in the United States and in Western Europe would never have reached the heights seen today. And rather than Central and Eastern Europe (and consequently half of the globe) falling into communist hands and for more than forty years being plundered, devastated, and forcibly insulated from Western markets, all of Europe (and the entire globe) would have remained integrated

economically (as in the nineteenth century) in a world-wide system of division of labor and cooperation. World living standards would have grown immensely higher than they actually have."[182]

In spite of infinite pronouncements to the contrary, we have every right to be skeptical about the progressive's desire for peace. How does one reconcile this purportedly sincere and intense desire for peace with the utter lack of interest in *defining* the term. When is the last time you heard anyone define the word "peace"?[183] If you don't know where you are going, you are unlikely to get there except by accident. Needless to say, the world has yet to stumble upon peace.

My suspicion is, even if the world pondered the question and was inexorably drawn to liberalism's common sense definition of peace — *the absence of violence or the palpable threat of violence against persons and their property including by the state*—progressives would recoil in horror at the prospect of such a world.

It's not that progressives don't like peace in general terms; it's just that *there are many things they value more highly*. Many of these things can only be achieved by the use of progressive state violence or the palpable threat of progressive state violence against persons and their property. *That is why we live in such a violent world*. We are lying in the bed we have made. Most people don't want peace, not really. If they did, it could be achieved without enormous difficulty since "there is no way to peace; peace is the way."[184]

---

[182] See, Hans-Hermann Hoppe, *Anarcho-Capitalism: An Annotated Bibliography*.

[183] J. Ostrowski, "The Myth of Democratic Peace: Why Democracy Cannot Deliver Peace in the 21st Century," *LewRockwell.com*, Feb. 19, 2005.

[184] A. J. Muste, "Debasing Dissent," *New York Times* (Nov. 16, 1967).

8. Progressivism as Utopianism

One element of the progressive mindset, utopianism, is important enough to merit extended treatment. Progressivism is a form of utopianism and shares all the defects of the utopian fallacy. Utopia means "an imaginary place in which the government, laws, and social conditions are perfect."[185] This dictionary definition is adequate for our purposes; however, it should be amended to make explicit what is implicit in the requirement of "perfection": no such place can possibly exist. In fact, the term, created by Saint Thomas More, means "no place" in Latin. Any model of society that contains essential elements that violate the laws of nature, logic, or economics, is utopian and therefore cannot exist in its intended form. The pursuit of impossible forms of society can only end badly and history confirms this.

Consider how progressivism manifests itself in everyday life. A problem occurs in the world such as a plane crash or a school shooting or a teenager bullied in government school commits suicide (problem "A"). The progressive mind immediately asks, how can government action solve that problem? The unstated assumptions are:

1. there is a solution to every human problem;
2. that solution can be discovered and imposed by the government to actually solve the problem; and
3. the governmental solution to the problem will be, in effect, cost-free and problem-free such that solving the initial problem will not involve the expenditure of important resources which are thereby rendered unavailable to solve other problems *and* will not cause any new problems. Thus, solving problem "A" will

---

[185] Merriam-Webster.

not lead to or cause new and additional problems "B",
"C", "D"......

I submit that all three premises are unproven, unsupported by any
evidence or logic and fall within the category of political dreams and
fantasies and are therefore utopian thinking. The entire progressive
program, however, essentially consists of applying those three
unproven premises to solve each and every human problem that arises
in the course of daily life.

Utopianism is worse than an idea that simply doesn't work.
Utopianism is an insidious political worldview because *it places a higher
value on a fantasy world than on existing human beings*.[186] The drug of utopia
desensitizes the utopian crusader to the harm his policies do to real
people. This may explain the progressive's callous disregard of the
immense human cost of progressive policy failures such as the welfare
state, public housing, government schools and the war on drugs. The
inner city of America is a dangerous wasteland filled with despair, yet,
the progressive not only unapologetically continues to urge that failed
progressive policies continue, but he doubles down on them,
demanding ever-increasing sums of money and ever more power.

Another consequence of utopianism is *ruthlessness*, a trait well
known among progressive politicians from Wilson through LBJ and
beyond. The feeling is, when you are making a utopian omelet, you
can break a few eggs, to paraphrase Walter Duranty's famous
exculpation of Stalin.

Utopianism also explains the sanctimoniousness of progressives
and their demonization of political opponents. After all, when one
side's goal is to replicate heaven on earth, those who oppose them
must be evil, depraved miscreants.

Finally, the utopian element of progressivism leads in the direction
of totalitarianism. Progressivism is naturally inclined to create a total

---

[186] Cf., Courtois. "Marxism-Leninism deified the system itself, so that
categories and abstractions were far more important than any human
reality." Stéphane Courtois and Mark Kramer, *The Black Book of
Communism: Crimes, Terror, Repression* (Harvard University Press, 1999),
p. 752.

state as it has no limiting principle to start with. Combine that natural inclination with the ultimate moral sanction of solving all human problems by means of state force and you have a potent formula for creeping totalitarianism. It is true that progressivism does not present a final vision of utopia like Marx did. It is, admittedly a piecemeal utopia wherein each human problem is "solved" in turn. That simply means that instead of the total state being installed instantaneously as the Bolsheviks did, progressive totalitarianism is being installed piece by piece while we sleep. We hardly notice it but one day you may wake up and find that your life is entirely under state control from dawn to dusk and thereafter and there is nothing you can do about it.

9. A Rogue's Gallery of Progressives

The popular image of progressivism is one of a benevolent and humanitarian movement led by secular saints solely motivated by love of people. That myth is belied by a close look at the main heroes of progressivism. True, villains may still produce good and true ideas. Philosophers have identified the fallacious *argument ad Hitlerum*: "Hitler believed X; therefore X must be false." Nevertheless, a brief glimpse into the lives and character of major progressive or proto-progressive figures will still be useful. I have already demonstrated that progressive ideas are false and destructive. Thus, it will be illuminating to see that such ideas sprang from dubious and questionable and power-hungry actors. You shall know the tree by the fruit it bears. But you can also know the fruit by the tree that bore it.

Every progressive policy involves the decision to use deadly physical force against those who refuse to comply with the policy. Progressives either know that, explicitly or implicitly, or are so unconscious about the actual facts of how governments operate, that their blissful ignorance amounts to a reckless and callous indifference to the plight of the victims of the policies they actively support and promote. Thus, there is something intrinsically evil about progressivism. It should then be no surprise that many of its main proponents and heroes were odious characters.

Abraham Lincoln. Discussing Lincoln, Rothbard identified a common characteristic of the progressive reform type and adopted Isabel Patterson's ingenious term, "humanitarian with a guillotine":

> "An ambitious seeker of the main chance from early adulthood, Lincoln acted viciously toward his own humble frontier family in Kentucky. He abandoned his

151

fiancé in order to marry a wealthier Mary Todd, whose family were friends of the eminent Henry Clay, he repudiated his brother, and he refused to attend his dying father or his father's funeral, monstrously declaring that such an experience 'would be more painful than pleasant.' No doubt!

"Lincoln, too, was a typical example of a humanitarian with the guillotine in another dimension: a familiar modern 'reform liberal' type whose heart bleeds for and yearns to "uplift" remote mankind, while he lies to and treats abominably actual people whom he knew. And so Abraham Lincoln, in a phrase prefiguring our own beloved Mario Cuomo, declared that the Union was really 'a family, bound indissolubly together by the most intimate organic bonds.' Kick your own family, and then transmute familial spiritual feelings toward a hypostatized and mythical entity, 'The Union,' which then must be kept intact regardless of concrete human cost or sacrifice."

The post-assassination veneration of Lincoln as a secular saint has bamboozled generations of Americans as to his actual life story. Professor Thomas DiLorenzo has authored two works on Lincoln that take a more realistic and factual approach.[187] I once made a list of DiLorenzo's criticisms or observations about Lincoln or his subordinates in order to show that his numerous critics had failed to rebut them:

1. Saying contradictory things before different audiences.
2. Opposing racial equality.

---

[187] *The Real Lincoln: A New Look at Abraham Lincoln, His Agenda, and an Unnecessary War,* Prima (2002); *Lincoln Unmasked: What You're Not Supposed to Know About Dishonest Abe,* Crown Forum (2006).

3. Opposing giving blacks the right to vote, serve on juries or intermarry while allegedly supporting their natural rights.

4. Being a racist.

5. Supporting the legal rights of slaveholders.

6. Supporting Clay's American System or mercantilism as his primary political agenda: national bank, high tariff, and internal improvements.

7. Supporting a political economy that encourages corruption and inefficiency.

8. Supporting a political economy that became the blueprint for modern America.

9. Being a wealthy railroad lawyer.

10. Never defending a runaway slave.

11. Defending a slaveholder against his runaway slave.

12. Favoring returning ex-slaves to Africa or sending them to Central America and Haiti.

13. Proposing to strengthen the Fugitive Slave law.

14. Opposing the extension of slavery in the territories so that "free white people" can settle there and because allowing them to become slave states would dilute Republican influence in Congress because of the three-fifths rule.

15. Opposing black citizenship in Illinois or their right to immigrate to that state.

16. Failing to use his legendary political skills to achieve peaceful emancipation as was accomplished elsewhere—Lincoln's war was the only "war of emancipation" in the 19th century.

17. Nullifying emancipation of slaves in Missouri and Georgia early in the war.

18. Stating that his primary motive was saving the union and not ending slavery.

19. Supporting a conscription law.

20. Sending troops into New York City to quell draft riots related to his Emancipation Proclamation, resulting in 300 to 1,000 deaths.

21. Starting a war that took the lives of 620,000 soldiers and 50,000 civilians and caused incalculable economic loss.
22. Being an enemy of free market capitalism.
23. Being an economic illiterate and espousing the labor theory of value.
24. Supporting a disastrous public works project in Illinois and continuing to support the same policies oblivious of the consequences.
25. Conjuring up a specious and deceptive argument against the historically-recognized right of state secession.
26. Lying about re-supplying the fed's tax collection office known as Fort Sumter.
27. Refusing to see peace commissioners from the Confederacy offering to pay for all federal property in the South.
28. Refusing to see Napoleon III of France who offered to mediate the dispute.
29. Provoking Virginia to secede by taking military action against the Deep South.
30. Supporting a tariff and other policies that systematically redistributed wealth from the South to the North, causing great consternation in the South.
31. Invading the South without consulting Congress.
32. Illegally declaring martial law.
33. Illegally blockading ports.
34. Illegally suspending habeas corpus.
35. Illegally imprisoning thousands of Northern citizens.
36. Tolerating their subjection to inhumane conditions in prison.
37. Systematically attacking Northern newspapers and their employees, including by imprisonment.
38. Deporting his chief political enemy in the North, Congressman Clement L. Vallandigham of Ohio.
39. Confiscating private property and firearms.
40. Ignoring the Ninth and Tenth Amendments.

41. Tolerating the arrest of ministers who refused to pray for Lincoln.
42. Arresting several duly elected members of the Maryland Legislature along with the mayor of Baltimore and Maryland Congressman Henry May.
43. Placing Kansas and Kentucky under martial law.
44. Supporting a law that indemnified public officials for unlawful acts.
45. Laying the groundwork for the establishment of conscription and income taxation as permanent institutions.
46. Interfering with and rigging elections in Maryland and elsewhere in the North.
47. Censoring all telegraph communication.
48. Preventing opposition newspapers from being delivered by the post office.
49. Illegally creating the state of West Virginia out of the "indestructible" state of Virginia.
50. Tolerating or supporting mistreatment of citizens in conquered territory.
51. Taxing those citizens without their consent.
52. Executing those who refused to take a loyalty oath.
53. Closing churches and arresting ministers.
54. Burning and plundering Southern cities.
55. Quartering troops in private homes unlawfully.
56. Creating an enormous political patronage system.
57. Allowing an unjust mass execution of Sioux Indians in Minnesota.
58. Engineering a constitutional revolution through military force which destroyed state sovereignty and replaced it with rule by the Supreme Court (and the United States Army).
59. Laying the groundwork for the imperialist and militarist campaigns of the future as well as the welfare/warfare state.

60. Creating the dangerous precedent of establishing a strong consolidated state out of a decentralized confederation.
61. Effectively killing secession as a threat, thus encouraging the rise of our modern federal monolith.
62. Waging war on civilians by bombing, destruction of homes, and confiscation of food and farm equipment.
63. Tolerating an atmosphere which led to large numbers of rapes of Southern women, including slaves.
64. Using civilians as hostages.
65. Promoting a general because of his willingness to use his troops as cannon fodder.
66. DiLorenzo blames Lincoln for the predictable aftermath of the war: the plundering of the South by Lincoln's allies.
67. Supporting government subsidies of the railroads leading to corruption and inefficiency.
68. Supporting a nationalized paper currency which is inherently inflationary.
69. Creating the federal tax bureaucracy and various taxes that are still with us.
70. Establishing precedents for centralized powers and suppression of liberties that continue to be cited today.
71. Ending slavery by means that created turbulence that continues to this day.

Lincoln created the template for future progressive presidents. He greatly expanded the powers of government in domestic affairs. Those expanded powers were justified by reference to the common good but in reality they served the interests of big business and the plutocacrcy. He was almost uniformly hostile to civil liberties. Finally, he launched one of the major wars in modern history in the fervent belief that war can improve society, which proposition is simply a species of the general progressive proposition that the use of aggressive government force can improve society.

Teddy Roosevelt. Lincoln created the template for progressive presidents but that was before the formal era of Progressivism and

Lincoln himself led us to believe that he was not making a break from the Founding Fathers but was merely fulfilling their promises. It was left to Teddy Roosevelt to announce that Lincoln was the first progressive president and the polar opposite of the author of the Declaration of Independence whom TR loathed. Roosevelt, however, was far more important as an advocate for expansive government and war than an actual perpetrator of those foul deeds.

The beginning of the Progressive Era coincides with the terms of three progressive presidents, Theodore Roosevelt (1901-1908); William Howard Taft (1909-1912); and Woodrow Wilson (1913-1920). Progressive thought had been developing in the prior decades particularly with the pragmatists; but now the movement had achieved power and began to execute its platform. America would never be the same.

Though Roosevelt was the founding father of Progressivism, later presidents including Wilson, Franklin Roosevelt, and Lyndon Johnson helped create the progressive state that exists today with lesser figures such as the Bushes and Barack Obama adding important elements of the ever-growing progressive state.

The story of how Roosevelt got on the ticket with William McKinley in 1900 is told by Murray Rothbard and it illustrates an important truth about progressivism. As Rudyard Kipling wrote about British progressivism, "All is not Gold that Glitters."[188] Progressivism is both a sincerely-held belief system and an ideology that is extremely useful in manipulating the masses to support policies that benefit discrete, secretive and powerful private interests.

Rothbard writes:

> "William McKinley reflected the dominance of the Republican Party by the Rockefeller/Standard Oil interests. Standard Oil was originally headquartered at Rockefeller's home in Cleveland, and the oil magnate had long had a commanding influence in Ohio Republican politics. In the early 1890s, Marcus Hanna, industrialist and high school chum of John D.

---

[188] "The Gods of the Copybook Headings."

Rockefeller, banded together with Rockefeller and other financiers to save McKinley from bankruptcy, and Hanna became McKinley's top political adviser and chairman of the Republican National Committee. As a consolation prize to the Morgan interests for McKinley's capture of the Republican nomination, Morgan man Garret A. Hobart, director of various Morgan companies, including the Liberty National Bank of New York City, became Vice-President. The death of Hobart in 1899 led to a "Morgan vacancy" in the Vice-Presidential spot, as McKinley walked into the nomination. McKinley and Hanna were both hostile to Roosevelt, considering him "erratic" and a "Madman," but after several Morgan men turned down the nomination, and after the intensive lobbying of Morgan partner George W. Perkins, Teddy Roosevelt at last received the Vice-Presidential nomination. It is not surprising that virtually Teddy's first act after the election of 1900 was to throw a lavish dinner in honor of J. P. Morgan."

Out of office, TR played a pioneering role in enacting the federal income tax, the funding mechanism of the progressive welfare-warfare state ever since.[189] TR helped create the modern imperial presidency by starting the tradition of issuing executive orders.[190] As Jim Powell wrote, TR "established a new model of aggressive American intervention abroad."[191] He favored the theft of Hawaii.[192] He worked hard to bring about a war in Cuba.[193] One of the finest Americans who ever lived, Mark Twain, saw clearly that TR was a dangerous maniac.[194]

---

[189] *Bully Boy: The Truth About Theodore Roosevelt's Legacy*, Crown Forum, N. Y. (2006), p. 230.

[190] *Id.* at 4.

[191] *Id.* at 8.

[192] *Id.* at 44.

[193] *Id.* at 52.

[194] Edmund Morris, *The Rise of Theodore Roosevelt* (2001), Prologue.

Understanding nothing about economics, he stomped like a bully through the china shop of the American economy, waging war against efficient business firms including the railroads that had created the most vibrant economy in world history and cut prices of essential goods for the masses.[195] He was usually allied with special interest groups and against the interests of the average American. He pretended, however, to be on the side of the common man. "I am for men, not for property," he said. This echoes the modern idiotic progressive slogan, "people over profits." TR's formulation implies that men are somehow floating in space and need no property to live. Yet, his statement is literally a lie: his support of the income tax proves that he was *for property*, government property controlled by him. The brilliant liberal Mark Twain had his number. He called Roosevelt "far and away the worst President we have ever had." Of course, this was before Woodrow Wilson had his turn.

Woodrow Wilson. Woodrow Wilson was our worst president. He did many of the things that Lincoln did to destroy life, liberty and property but did them on a grander scale, with less excuse and with more lasting consequences. It is true that Lincoln laid the groundwork for the modern monstrosity we suffer under now, however, it is also true that federal spending sharply declined after his war and remained modest until the Wilson administration. It was *Wilson*, not Lincoln, who birthed the permanent federal leviathan of today.

Lincoln's war was brutal and savage and its damage is still felt today, however, at least his apologists have resort to the *post hoc* rationalization that he was "freeing the slaves." In pushing the United States into the war that would ruin a human century, Wilson was instead freeing the British and French Empires. Enormous egos typify the leaders of progressivism: TR, FDR, LBJ. None of them, however, recklessly plunged our nation into a world war in the absence of a direct attack, believing that the resulting chaos would somehow reshape the world for the better. Don't let his utter lack of charisma fool you. Wilson's ego was as big as any of theirs.

Wilson's various contributions to big government surpass those of any other president. They include:

---

[195] *Id.* at 120, et seq.

A Rogues' Gallery of Progressives

1. The twin funding sources of progressive government, the income tax and the Federal Reserve.
2. The war on drugs—the Harrison Act of 1914.
3. Participation in a world war that continues to cause international chaos to this very day (e.g., Iraq, Syria).
4. The institution of "war socialism"[196] wherein the government asserted the right to seize control of the economy to aid the war effort.[197]
5. The ultimate evil of conscription wherein state officials claim the right to seize your body, transport it to places you never heard of and pointlessly kill it at their own whim.
6. "He ordered unconstitutional, unilateral military interventions into Haiti, the Dominican Republic, and Mexico. (He also oversaw military interventions in Panama and Cuba, and instituted American-favored dictators throughout Latin America.)"[198]
7. Massive and grotesque civil liberties violations that have been largely forgotten because all those who suffered through them are now dead. This was typified by the jailing of Eugene V. Debs for speaking out against the war and the draft. Wilson denied the ailing Debs' request for clemency.[199]

---

[196] R. Raico, "World War I on the Home Front," *Mises Daily*, Oct. 12, 2012.

[197] Higgs, *Crisis and Leviathan, pp.* 128–29.

[198] R. Balko, "What's Wrong With Woodrow Wilson?" *Reason.com*, Oct. 11, 2010.

[199] "It took Warren Harding, one of the 'worst' American Presidents according to numerous polls of history professors, to pardon Debs, when Wilson, a 'Near-Great,' would have let him die a prisoner. Debs and 23 other jailed dissidents were freed on Christmas Day, 1921. To

A Rogues' Gallery of Progressives

Like the other four major progressive presidents discussed in this chapter, Wilson was hostile to liberty across the board, favoring war as a positive good, central economic planning and massive violations of civil liberties such as free speech. While the other four all made great strides towards expanding state power and shrinking liberty, none was as successful as Wilson in destroying liberty.

FDR. Franklin D. Roosevelt is the patron saint of progressivism. It is as it must be. The progressive state was not fully constructed under Lincoln. The same is true with TR plus he had that crazed look in his eye. Mark Twain thought he was "clearly insane."[200] Wilson did make a great leap forward into progressivism but he was too cerebral and lacked charisma and had no sense of humor. Skipping past FDR, LBJ obviously fails the saint test (see below) and looked like a villain. The only real candidate for progressive sainthood is FDR. He had charisma, a pleasant, grandfatherly visage, had overcome a serious illness, and, as the myth goes, got us out of the Depression and saved us from the Germans (who couldn't even get an army across the twenty-one mile wide English Channel).

Since the progressives have canonized FDR, it is imperative that this saint be defrocked. Saint Franklin was a scoundrel in both his private and public lives. He was a serial adulterer and illegally spied on his wife's own dalliances.[201] Lying was second nature to him. He covered up his serious health problems to get elected to an unprecedented fourth term. He called one of history's worst villains, Stalin, "Uncle Joe," had a warm relationship with him and covered up his infamous massacre of 22,000 Polish Army officers and prominent

---

those who praised him for his clemency, Harding replied: 'I couldn't do anything else.... Those fellows didn't mean any harm. It was a cruel punishment.'" Ralph Raico, *Great Wars and Great Leaders*, Ludwig von Mises, 2010, p. 42.

[200] "TR: Political Tom Sawyer".

[201] C. McGrath, "No End of the Affair," *NYTimes*, April 20, 2008.

citizens.[202] Several close associates of FDR were communists or communist sympathizers.[203] FDR conspired to get us into war with Japan while pretending to be a peace candidate.

FDR used tactics more popularly associated with Richard Nixon. He used the IRS to punish political enemies.[204] He illegally wiretapped political opponents. He illegally closed the banks under color of a war power but in peacetime.[205] FDR, not Goldfinger, was the biggest gold thief of all time. He was guilty of war crimes, a consistent theme with progressive presidential heroes.[206]

But let's not forget his more mundane failures. Contrary to myth, FDR didn't get the country out of the Great Depression. Rather, he stupidly extended it and worsened it, causing immense human suffering in the process. As economist Thomas DiLorenzo noted, unemployment remained high throughout the New Deal. Nor did the war end the Depression. The economy only recovered after the war ended.[207] The war gave the appearance of recovery with millions of men shipped overseas and factories busy making weapons of mass destruction, however, there was little to buy on the domestic front and price controls created chronic shortages. Your local mobster could get you rationing coupons for a premium.

---

[202] "Declassified documents prove U.S. DID help cover up 1940 Katyn massacre where Soviets slaughtered 22,000 Polish officers," *Associated Press*, Sept. 10, 2012.

[203] Thomas E. Woods, *The Politically Incorrect Guide to American History* Regnery Publishing Inc., Washington, D.C. 2004), pp. 157 et seq.; Jim Powell, *FDR's Folly: How Roosevelt and His New Deal Prolonged the Great Depression*, Three Rivers Press, NY (2003), p. 15.

[204] G. Chadduck, "Playing the IRS card: Six presidents who used the IRS to bash political foes," *SCMonitor.com*, May 17, 2013.

[205] Jim Powell, *supra* at 53, et seq.

[206] D. Larison, "FDR's Crimes," *AmericanConservative.com*, May 13, 2005.

[207] T. DiLorenzo, "Franklin Delano Roosevelt's New Deal: From Economic Fascism to Pork-Barrel Politics," in *Reassessing the Presidency: The Rise of the Executive State and the Decline of Freedom* (Mises Institute, 2001), pp. 425-426.

A Rogues' Gallery of Progressives

The New Deal was a jumble of contradictory, crackpot ideas which replaced voluntary market relations with government coercion. These included massive tax increases, empowering labor unions to extract above-market wages and thus create unemployment and underemployment for non-union workers, the creation of monopolies throughout the economy, price controls and the destruction of crops and farm animals to boost food prices while people were destitute.[208]

When all his idiotic economic policies had failed, FDR got bored with the domestic front and turned his attention to the European war. While lying to the voters at home about staying out of the war, he actively conspired with Churchill and Stalin to drag America into the quagmire. Keep in mind that the progressive is a pragmatist and a pragmatist defines truth as that which works. That explains why FDR could and would and did lie without compunction. What the pragmatist leaves out of the formula is this: *lying to get what we want is manipulative of others.* It involves negating the minds of others as guides to their own conduct of affairs by providing them with false information. It is, to use a term a pragmatist would scoff at, morally wrong. It is also arrogant, involving the delusion of special powers to predict the future. It involves a denial of the primordial condition of man: ignorance about the future.

We are almost entirely ignorant about the future consequences of war, yet progressive icons are to this very day lauded for their decisions to plunge the nation into massive continental and world wars whose immediate, intermediate and long-range consequences were largely unknown at the time. For example, in Wilson's defense, it can be argued that he did not know that dragging the United States into World War I made the rise of a Hitler more likely. Yet, defending Wilson's decision to wage war by boasting of his ignorance of the consequences seems like more of an indictment on a different charge. Thus, the progressive's blind faith in aggressive government action in war is similar to their blind faith in aggressive government action in the economy or social life: based on nothing but air.

LBJ. Lyndon Baines Johnson is the prototype of the egomaniacal, sociopathic progressive politician. Nevertheless, he remains a hero to

---

[208] See generally, Jim Powell, *supra.*

progressives for his alleged domestic accomplishments such as socialized medicine. The fact that there is no proof that Medicare and Medicaid improved overall health in America doesn't faze them, illustrating once again that progressivism is not a rational or scientific system of thought but a form of emotional therapy. The notion that such a proposition needed to be proven probably never occurred to them. According to charts of 20th century American health statistics, the enactment of Medicare and Medicaid in the late 1960's appears to have had zero positive affect on American health. Nor are LBJ's admirers bothered by the massive failure of Johnson's war on poverty and the present state of inner city America as a wasteland.

LBJ is the perfect symbol of the ugly reality of progressivism. He increased government power in all three policy sectors, the economy, civil liberties and foreign policy. He escalated the Vietnam conflict into a full-scale war to protect his right flank from criticism for being soft on communism. A million people died and tens of thousands were maimed so this scoundrel could maintain power. He was a corrupt, unstable, egotistical bully and utterly oblivious to the suffering his policies caused. Rather, he reportedly spent much of the time feeling sorry for *himself* because Vietnam ended his presidency.[209] He left the inner city of America and Vietnam in a shambles. He was a career criminal, whether judged by the standards of natural law or positive (government) law. He illegally wiretapped his political opponents including MLK. He was not only a serial adulterer and harasser of his secretarial pool but he boasted of his exploits.[210] He lied about staying out of the Vietnam War and accused Goldwater of being the warmonger. He dropped the N-word frequently.[211] Racism against blacks and lying about staying out of war seems to be standard operating procedure among the progressive Presidents (except for TR).

---

[209] See, Helen Thomas & Craig Crawford, *Listen Up, Mr. President: Everything You Always Wanted Your President to Know and Do*, Scribner, 2009, p. 83.

[210] See, Ronald Kessler, *In the President's Secret Service*, pp. 15-17.

[211] quod.lib.umich.edu/l/lincoln.

A Secret Service agent assigned to his detail thought to himself, "If Johnson weren't president, he'd be in an insane asylum."[212]

It cannot be said in defense of progressivism that the problem with LBJ is that he was an odious character who just happened into power and that the system would work well if a better sort was elected. There is no guarantee that a better sort will be elected and in fact there is a natural tendency for the worst to get to the top as Hayek and others have argued.[213] Evil sorts will tend to gravitate toward arbitrary power since *arbitrary power is intrinsically evil.* Good people will shy away precisely because they are good and have no use for arbitrary power. LBJ was not an aberration of progressivism but its apotheosis.

Conclusion. Men and women who seek to improve the human condition have a basic choice. Their tool can either be truth or novelty. Often the truth has already been discovered by the great figures of the past and thus there is usually no reason to reinvent the wheel. Yet, to those with colossal egos, this may be unsatisfactory. Megalomaniacs are usually not content to recycle the wisdom of the past even if true and they often lack the ability to make new discoveries that add to true human knowledge. What is a megalomaniac to do?

Overthrowing the past offers the potential for greater glory even if such revolutionary ideas are evil, baseless and destructive. The temptation can be irresistible. The history of progressivism is strewn with figures with colossal egos but modest talents beyond power-seeking. History shows that evil deeds often arise from a gross disparity between ego and achievement (Evil = Ego/Achievement). The egomaniac is willing to plunge nations into war for power or glory or fame. The rogues described in this chapter did achieve historical fame while callously ignoring the costs including endless piles of human corpses, the devastation of the inner cities of America and the sabotaging of the most important political achievement in recorded human history: liberalism.

---

[212] Ronald Kessler, *In the President's Secret Service: Behind the Scenes with Agents in the Line of Fire and the President They Protect*, Crown Forum, 2009.

[213] "Why the Worst Get on Top," chapter ten of *The Road to Serfdom.*

10. How to Bury Progressivism and Restore American Liberty

"Be courageous! …. Be brave . . . Have faith and
go forward!"

~Thomas Alva Edison

Step one in burying the most destructive idea ever taken seriously in America, progressivism, was to identify and define the idea itself and attach a word to it. See Chapter 1. That critical step had never to my knowledge been done in an accessible manner and in booklet form for mass distribution. Step two is understanding the destructive role progressivism has played in American history for longer than any of us has been alive. See Chapters 2-9. Step three is formulating and executing a strategy for defeating progressivism.

It is hard to defeat an opponent that is nameless. Many progressives don't use the term to describe themselves though some do. They often don't use *any* word to describe themselves. Their opponents usually call them "liberals." In turn, the term many of their opponents use to describe themselves, "conservative," is ill-defined or is understood to mean a variety of things, often mutually contradictory. This linguistic confusion must change if progressivism is to be defeated.

I propose the following changes of terminology:

1. Instead of "liberal," call those who believe in big government "progressives."

2. Instead of "libertarian," call those who support voluntary social relations "liberals."
3. Draw a sharp demarcation between conservatives and libertarians, now "liberals."

"Liberal" to *"progressive."* This is really a no-brainer. "Progressive" is the word that contemporary "liberals" often call themselves. Today's "liberals" hate to use the word "liberal" since their foes have made it into a dirty word over the last several decades. They have abandoned the term. Calling them small "p" progressives also connects them to the Progressive Era they proudly accept as their heritage. On the other hand, progressives never should have been called liberals in the first place.

"Libertarian" to *"liberal."* The loss of the word "liberal" left the Liberty Movement without a label. Contrary to popular belief, labels are good, not bad. They are in fact indispensable. If you lack a label in politics, you might as well not exist. The founders of the modern resurgence of the Liberty Movement understood that and decided on the term "libertarian." Fair enough. However, though etymologically correct, the term has not served the movement well.

"Libertarian" is one syllable too many and has an esoteric academic feel for a term that represents something uncomplicated, individual liberty. Hayek called it "singularly unattractive. For my taste it carries too much the flavor of a manufactured term and of a substitute."[214] It is easily confused with the pre-existing term "civil libertarian," which is often associated with progressives. Worst of all, as a neologism, it necessarily cuts off the Liberty Movement from its ancient and glorious history. It is true that the word "libertarian" appears in history in the 19th century as referring to one who favors individual liberty, but its use was not popular nor were major movements favoring liberty popularly or historically known as "libertarian."

Cut off from history and suggesting something entirely new, the term "libertarian" facilitates critics who believe the movement is a new cult of some kind. In the early days of the movement, there was a

---

[214] "Why I am Not a Conservative."

persistent belief among many that libertarians were associated with Lyndon Larouche. This is probably because the Libertarian Party was a third party and the best known third party presidential candidate was Lyndon Larouche. Yikes! A final reason for abandoning the term "libertarian" is its unfortunate association with the failed conservative movement.

Since the term "liberal" was misappropriated by those who are hostile to liberty and those people no longer use the word to describe themselves, *it is time to take the word back*. If that can be accomplished, the Liberty Movement would have a short, beautiful word that is etymologically correct and reconnects the movement with its glorious past.

"Conservative" ≠ "libertarian." The Liberty Movement must make a clean break from the failed and hopeless conservative movement. Conservatives have had 50 years on the national stage and have failed to defeat progressivism or advance liberty in any significant way. None of the Liberty Movement's temporary alliances with conservatives bore fruit. These include the election of Ronald Reagan, the so-called Republican Revolution of 1994 and the Tea Party movement of 2009-2010. In each cause, libertarians were treated as a junior partner. Conservatives were happy to have the libertarians' energy, brains, money and votes. But in each case, after gaining power, the libertarian agenda was tossed aside and the libertarians were forgotten completely.

Finally, the Ron Paul presidential campaign of 2012 was an acid test of whether conservatives would support a libertarian cause. Long story short—they didn't. Even though Ron Paul courted conservatives, few conservatives supported him, apparently because of his limited government foreign policy views. Libertarian efforts to court conservatives have failed. Conservatives themselves have failed to shrink government when they had the chances. Yet, the left attacks conservative politicians for their *alleged* free market philosophy anyway. For all these reasons, the Liberty Movement must separate from those who are not consistent defenders of liberty lest we be tainted. Conveniently, adopting the term "liberal" will only assist in that separation.

Strategy is the Achilles Heel of the Liberty Movement. The "Liberty Movement" refers to the modern rebirth of classical liberalism in the late 1960's after its virtual extinction from about 1900 through the 1960's. The Liberty Movement has been remarkably successful in producing a valuable body of liberal scholarship, creating a sizable cadre of hardcore activists and expanding its level of support among the public to as much as ten percent as evidenced by the Ron Paul for President campaigns. The Liberty Movement has failed, however, in developing a strategy to actually move the country toward liberty and away from progressive big government. In fact, government has steadily grown in size, scope and power throughout the duration of the Liberty Movement and while the Liberty Movement has undeniably grown and expended considerable amounts of money each year. Lack of good strategies not only guarantees failure but harms the movement by causing burnout in activists by having them expend time, energy and money pointlessly.

State of the Liberty Movement. Is there a Liberty Movement? At times, it seems like there are a million tiny and ineffective liberty movements. There is no one leader or group in charge of the movement and the very thought of such a leader would be anathema to movement activists who chafe at top-down modes of organization. The term "Liberty Movement" is as much a prayer as a description of facts on the ground. This is particularly true in the post-Ron Paul presidential campaign era. From late 2007 through 2012, the two campaigns *were* the Liberty Movement. In my view, the energy level of the Movement since he ceased his last campaign—his own son's endorsement of the *progressive* Republican Mitt Romney is a good demarcation—has declined by many magnitudes. Others in the movement may disagree and it's largely a matter of perspective.

I do *not* regularly attend Liberty Movement events as I am busy with the day job and family life. I am also in the belly of the progressive beast, Buffalo, New York. Most of my contacts in life and in politics are with people outside the movement. Mine is a real world perspective. It cannot be denied that the Ron Paul campaigns energized grass roots activists all over the country and even in Buffalo where 700 people attended a rally on short notice. In the aftermath of the campaigns, this activism was not replaced by anything remotely resembling the magnitude of the Ron Paul Revolution.

How to Bury Progressivism and Restore American Liberty

A word about the debate over movement strategy and tactics. There is a line of thought in the movement that says that any and all strategies and tactics are equally valid and should not be criticized. That is nonsense in my view. All strategies and tactics use scarce resources that are therefore unavailable to be applied towards other strategic and tactical ideas. *Using bad strategies hurts the movement.* That's why I have now written three books urging the movement to adopt better strategies and tactics than the ones that have been failing for over forty years to roll back the state. To be clear, I am not saying that the ideas I promote are the only valuable ideas the movement should be pursuing. What I am saying is that they are valuable ideas that have been underutilized and that can advance the goals of the movement more efficiently and quickly than other approaches that have been tried and failed many times.

1. *Talk to progressives.*

Libertarians have spent most of the last 40 years talking to each other. We love to attend seminars and conferences and political conventions and socialize with our comrades. It's fun and there's nothing wrong with fun. However, in a country where ninety percent of the people are progressives, simple mathematics tells us this strategy must fail. *We must directly engage our fellow citizens who do not share our worldview.* It would be great if there was a billionaire out there who would fund such an outreach program. Alas, there is not. It would be great if there was an organization that could do so. In fact, I know of no such organization. Nor do I have the wherewithal to create one myself. Rather, this effort has to be undertaken by individuals in the movement. Their efforts can be chronicled at LibertyMovement.org and perhaps the sum total of these efforts can be tracked so that activists can be assured that they are not working alone and that real progress is being made across the land. At the end of the day, however, the effort will succeed only if committed individuals take action and sustain it. I'm afraid there is no easier alternative.

After you read this book, make a list of ten friends and family members who are progressives. Loan your book to one of them and ask them to read it. Then, have breakfast with them and discuss the ideas in the book. Urge them to join the Liberty Movement for the good of the nation and their own good as well. Each month, lend the book to another friend or relative and go through the same process. This approach does not involve the expenditure of large sums of money or the need to make regular donations to organizations with little assurance that your money is being spent productively. This approach does not involve attending endless meetings and rallies that never seem to accomplish anything. It's a user-friendly approach and will allow you to catch up with folks you don't see enough of in today's busy world.

Other approaches have been tried. Political campaigns can on occasion lead to media coverage. The problem is, most reporters are progressives and they tend to give a progressive spin to campaign coverage. The Liberty Movement has a solid presence on the web; however, we tend to be reaching other members of the movement, not those we need to reach. Meetings, seminars, conventions and conferences all have their place but again, at such events, we are preaching to the choir. *Person-to-person outreach to people we know is the best approach available that has not been tried yet in any systematic way.*

If you don't have a book handy and happen to start up a conversation with a stranger about politics, give them a copy of the flier entitled, "Progressivism is Bad for Progressives." It is available on LibertyMovement.org. This should get a very interesting conversation going. The flier makes the case that holding progressive views is bad for progressives *themselves* for the following reasons:

1. Progressivism is in fact destroying the country we all live in and the country your children and grandchildren will inherit.
2. Progressivism gives us a false sense of control over our lives.
3. Progressivism fails to solve the problems we need solved; it merely pretends to do so.
4. Progressivism's misguided solutions create ever more new problems that didn't exist before. First, progressivism does lots of harm.

5. Under progressivism, *you* are forced to suffer under all the misguided laws and policies put in place in kneejerk fashion to solve other people's problems.

6. Progressivism is irrational and promotes state violence. Supporting such a worldview does come with psychic costs, or, at the very least, requires *a suspension of critical thinking* to avoid coming to grips with the true nature of the mindset of progressivism.

7. Progressivism crowds out real solutions to problems by focusing time, energy and loads of money on misguided solutions.

8. Progressivism breeds a false sense of security that various products and services are "safe and effective," when in fact they are not. How many people underwent unnecessary surgeries, x-rays, vaccinations or drug treatments mistakenly relying on government-certified doctors and drugs when a more skeptical approach would have led to a different and better choice? The progressive mindset, which produces such policies in the first place, essentially blinds progressives to the notion that these policies do not work.

9. Progressives, because of their views, are much more likely to:
    a. Work for the government with these costs:
        (1) Failing to hand down a marketable trade or skill to your children
        (2) Leaving no family business for your children to carry on.
        (3) You will generally not be rewarded for good job performance or hard work as your salary is set by law or contract.
        (4) Your own boss is a bureaucrat so will tend to act like one, often subjecting *you* to arbitrary treatment or harassment with impunity.
        (5) Depending on the bureaucracy you work for, you will often find yourself in hostile interactions with citizens.

      (6) *Be honest.* Are you truly fulfilling your unique human potential in your government job?

  b. Send their kids to K-12 government schools with these costs: exposing your children to pervasive crime, sexual promiscuity, drug activity, bullying, political propaganda, bureaucracy and poor teachers who are almost impossible to fire.

  c. Get entangled with government programs such as welfare with these costs:

    (1) Dependency,

    (2) Loss of privacy and control,

    (3) Encouraging your kids to be dependent as opposed to self-reliant,

    (4) Selling yourself short,

    (5) Turning away from family and friends for help.

10. Progressivism preys on the weaknesses of people and encourages people not to believe in themselves.

11. Progressivism, with its belief in the ability of majoritarian government to do all that it desires, destroys objective morality, right and wrong.

2. *Talk to Christian progressives.*

77 percent of Americans call themselves Christians while as many as 90 percent are progressives as I have defined the term. Since progressivism is in many ways inconsistent with Christianity, there is a real and untapped potential to move people away from progressivism. There is a flier outlining these arguments at LibertyMovement.org. Please print out copies and hand them out to your Christian family members and friends. This should get some very interesting conversations going. Here is a summary of the main points:

1. Jesus never said anything about what the government should do. His message is what *you* should do.

2. Trying to carry out the message of the Gospels by means of state violence is a heresy.

3. Progressivism's highest moral principle is majority rule. That means that it overrides *any and all* Christian moral principles. No man can serve two masters. The two leading Christian philosophers, Aquinas and Augustine agreed: *Lex iniusta non est lex.* ("An unjust law is no law at all.") However, under progressivism, every law passed by the majority is just by definition.

4. *Government welfare is not Christian charity.* Jesus never said, love your neighbor by pointing a sword at your other neighbors to get their money.

5. The motivation of many to support welfare is anything but Christian including:
   a. buying off the poor so they don't revolt against a corrupt system of corporatism, and,
   b. making sure that *someone else* deals with the poor and their problems because we don't want to be bothered with them.

6. The Progressive State of America is fundamentally hostile to Christianity on a wide range of issues—welfare, schools, war and torture.[215]

7. Government schools were designed to be anti-Christian and they have worked very well in that regard.

3. Take your kids out of government school.

This is the most important action you can take to save America, not to mention your own kids. I wrote a book about it and can only summarize it here. See, *Government Schools Are Bad for Your Kids: What You Need to Know* (2009).

Government schools were not established out of any dire need for them but rather for a variety of crass religious, political and economic motives. They were not immaculately conceived but rather were born

---

[215] See, J. Redford, "Jesus Is an Anarchist (A free-market/libertarian anarchist, that is--otherwise what is called an anarcho-capitalist.)"

175

out of a toxic stew of religious absolutism, Prussian militarism, utopian socialist leveling and special interest greed and power lust.

Today, government schools are loaded with crime, bullying, drugs and sexual promiscuity. They indoctrinate students into a false view of American history, one that is invariably favorable to ever-expanding government.

It is a myth that parents can escape to the suburbs to avoid exposing their children to school crime. A study by the Manhattan Institute found virtually equal rates of delinquency in suburban schools. Government schools are unresponsive, self-serving bureaucracies that have to take eligible students even with criminal records, assuming they even know they have criminal records! They may even *want* to accept such students because they mean more state aid. Crime in government schools is in the nature of things. You get what you pay for.

Open and notorious and explicit sexual activity has also become a feature of daily life in government schools. Many government schools are turning into fornicatoriums featuring more and more sex, and less and less education.

Moving on to drugs, your local government high school is often the best drug store in town. One *suburban* high school in Upstate New York is nicknamed "Heroin High." Government schools are the key distribution point for illegal drugs in many communities. One study concluded that "80% of the nation's high school students and 44% of middle-schoolers have personally seen illegal drugs used or sold and/or students drunk or high on the grounds of their schools."[216] Another study warns that rates of illegal drug use are no lower in suburban schools.[217]

Why is the problem so bad? *Government schools are filled with people who don't want to be there and who are bored and alienated.* As we are constantly reminded by those who *defend* government schools: *they must take all students.* The fact that your kids spend six hours a day with fellow students subject to virtually no screening process is hardly a

---

[216] Salynn Boyles, "Parents Blind to Rising School Drug Use", *WebMD Medical News* (Aug. 16, 2007).

[217] J. P. Greene & G. Forster, *supra.*

recommendation. It is also difficult to discipline students. So doing involves a whole host of legal and bureaucratic procedures. In private schools, disruptive students can easily be expelled. In government schools, those in charge of student discipline are bureaucrats, not particularly responsive to parental or student concerns. Private school principals must be responsive or face closing their doors due to a lack of customers.

A word to the wise should be sufficient. If you send your child to a government school, they may learn more about chemistry than you could possibly imagine.

Psychotropic drugs. As many as six percent of students in some government high schools are taking psychotropic drugs.[218] Psychotropic drugs are powerful, mind-altering chemicals that can cause serious temporary and permanent side-effects. They are often given to bored students whose behavior disrupts classrooms. They are a method of control in a regime premised on control. *The use of drugs to control students is the natural consequence of a system that forces parents to send their children to school and forces the children to be there.* That's all the law can accomplish: guaranteeing their physical presence. It cannot guarantee they will show up ready to learn or be docile. That's where the drugs—chemical coercion—come in.

Sentencing your children to thirteen years in government school subjects them to running a gauntlet of endless assaults on their well-being.

There is an epidemic of bullying in the government schools. It is commonplace to point out that many bullies are themselves victims of bullying who merely pass it along to those who are weaker since they can't strike back at the strong. The irony of the government school, *the biggest bully of young people in America*, urging its victims to stop being bullies is completely lost on the bureaucrats.

Government schools are glorified daytime prisons operating in an atmosphere of legally-enforced nihilism which defaults into the pseudo-religion of hedonism. *The hedonistic atmosphere of government schools is a necessary reflection of the nature of those schools.* No reform is

---

[218] "U.S. Kids Take More Psychotropic Drugs Than Europeans," *Health.com*, Sept. 24, 2008.

possible because such reform would make government schools the opposite of what they are: private schools.

There is only one way out: **out!**

In a republic, the theory is that power proceeds from the people and the government is the people's agent and servant. However, when the government, through its control of the schools, is given the power to shape the political mindset of its own citizens, that master-servant relationship is turned upside down. *The government becomes the master, the citizen the servant,* first inside the classroom but eventually outside it too.

In light of the obvious propaganda function of government schools, it must be emphasized that on a wide range of critical subjects, government schools would appear to be incapable of providing proper instruction at all! These include all the subjects where political philosophy plays an obvious role: history, civics, politics, law, ethics, and economics. Economist Ludwig von Mises believed it was "impossible to deal with any chapter of history without taking a definite stand on . . . implied economic doctrines."[219] He added, "The party that operates the schools is in a position to propagandize its tenets and to disparage those of other parties."[220]

Eventually, we come to the present sad state where the vast majority of the American people are unaware of their own true history. Being unaware, and thinking that the current regime is the best of all possible worlds, they are utterly unequipped to deal with the harsh new reality that the regime is failing and the nation is in the process of economic collapse.

What historical points of view have been suppressed, ignored or disparaged in the government schools?—*Precisely those that would be extremely valuable to Americans right now to help us navigate out of the mess we are in.*

It is critical for American citizens to understand their own history. However, they get a skewed view of history when the government controls the schools. A proper study of history *must* include alternative views and not simply the views that happen to be favored by the regime that controls the schools. Students should be given unimpeded

---

[219] *Human Action: A Treatise on Economics* (Contemporary Books: Chicago, 3rd. Rev. ed., 1949) p. 877.
[220] *Id.*

access to information on controversial aspects of history so they can learn how to think for themselves and reach their own conclusions.

Currently, America is in a state of crisis caused by its global military empire, gigantic welfare state and the business cycle caused by the Federal Reserve. (On that evil institution, see Ron Paul's bestseller, *End the Fed.*) Yet, Americans are handicapped in dealing with these crises because few Americans know that the Federal Reserve causes a boom and bust cycle and that 9/11 was blowback for decades of Federal intervention into the Middle East.[221] Thus, they fall for doomed policies such as Bush's War on Terror and Obama's bailout of the auto industry.

Worse yet, spending on government schools has established a permanent and large source of funding and workers for progressive Democratic causes. For example, Clarence, New York, is an affluent suburb outside of Buffalo where Republicans far outnumber Democrats. However, the Clarence Teachers Association is an affiliate of the New York State United Teachers and the American Federation of Teachers, both of which heavily bankroll Democratic candidates. Money flows from the taxpayers to the school district to the teachers to the unions to the Democratic Party. Thus, Republican parents who send their children to Clarence schools, are, in effect, bankrolling the treasury and ground troops of the party they vehemently oppose. To paraphrase Lenin, the capitalists are giving the progressives the rope they need to hang them.

America was supposed to be a highly decentralized peaceful commercial republic based on individual freedom and strictly limited government that minded its own business and stayed out of foreign conflicts. Instead, it is a highly centralized and militarized global empire whose extensive control over every aspect of our daily lives is rationalized by a distorted concept of majority rule that would have horrified the Founders—*that majorities have a right to destroy individual liberty.*

We have gone from a nation founded on loyalty to principles, including *the right of revolution against tyranny*, to one founded on loyalty

---

[221] See, Chalmers Johnson, "Blowback," *The Nation* (Sept. 27, 2001).

to the government. Government schools are the foundation of big government in America.

The grand result of our experiment with government schools is a population ill-prepared to deal with the present crisis in America.

It is time to pull the plug while there is still a country worth saving.

4. Vote With Your Feet.

If you live in a state that lacks the freedom you need to pursue the American Dream, it may be time to *vote with your feet* and, in effect, cast the deciding vote for lower taxes and more liberty. Scholars Jason Sorens and William P. Ruger have performed a valuable service by ranking the fifty states by how much personal and economic freedom they allow their citizens.[222] The degree of freedom in education is heavily weighted in the study: "The reason we consider education regulations so critically important is that they affect the future course of liberty by affecting how and what the next generation is taught." Here are the winners:

Overall Freedom Ranking (2013)

1. North Dakota
2. South Dakota
3. Tennessee
4. New Hampshire
5. Oklahoma
6. Idaho
7. Missouri
8. Virginia
9. Georgia
10. Utah

---

[222] Freedom in the Fifty States: An Index of Personal and Economic Freedom (Mercatus Center, George Mason University, 2013).

How to Bury Progressivism and Restore American Liberty

Listed below are the ten *least free states*, states that tend to take your spare change in taxes and also allow less choice in K-12 education. The authors single out Hawaii, Washington State, and oddly enough, Tennessee, the seventh freest state, for having burdensome education regulations. Idaho and Indiana on the other hand allow much educational freedom.

41. Mississippi
42. West Virginia
43. Vermont
44. Maryland
45. Illinois
46. Rhode Island
47. Hawaii
48. New Jersey
49. California
50. New York

Jason Sorens helped found the Free State Project which seeks to persuade 20,000 citizens to move to New Hampshire and make it even freer than it is today. Their website is at FreeStateProject.org. All I can say is, what a great idea!

A less drastic option is moving to another *county* which could merely involve a move of a few miles. The Tax Foundation publishes a valuable report each year listing each county's property taxes. Even counties in high property tax states such as New York can vary widely in the level of property taxes. For example, the median property tax in Monroe County (Rochester), New York was $3,705 in 2008 but was only $3052 in neighboring Ontario County. The bottom line is, whether you are considering moving or buying your first home, think hard before moving into a high tax town, school district, county or state. By avoiding those places, you will not only save extra dollars but you will also send a badly needed message of change to high tax regimes.

Every time you take an action that reduces government spending you perform the critical task of starving the beast! Total government spending is about $6,400,000,000,000 each year. Let's assume for the sake of argument that the forces of big government directly spend one percent of their receipts or $64,000,000,000 each year maintaining and expanding their power. (That's probably an understatement.) That sum is derived, directly or indirectly from total spending. For example, a corporation that kicks back donations to politicians who secured a grant for the corporation, is clearly recycling the grant money for political contributions. Thus, we can derive this rule of thumb: every hundred dollars of government spending generates a dollar that is used to maintain and even grow the status quo.

So in the example above, each family moving out of overtaxed Monroe County deprives "the machine" of $6.50 they could spend on donations, lobbying and government propaganda such as government school "history" classes. That may seem like a trivial amount, but it's not. If we can multiply that savings by millions of other Patriots making similar decisions on every level of government, we will have starved the beast of billions of dollars!

Now, look at the other side of equation. How much money does the Liberty Movement spend each year? My estimate is about one hundred million each year. Let's compare what "we" spend to what "they" spend. The difference is astounding. We are outspent 640 to one! So, don't dismiss small acts of starving the beast of a mere ten dollars when we only have one cent to match it.

5. Jury nullification.

The original Patriots did not trust government, including prosecutors or judges. They knew the only way to restrain the power of government was by *external* checks and balances. They gave us two: the right to bear arms and juries. Naturally, the government has tried to take both of these rights away from us.

The original concept of a jury was that it could override the judge on matters of law. Call that *jury nullification.* Every prominent founder who was a lawyer stated explicitly that juries have the right to judge the law itself and whether it would be unjust to convict a defendant for violating that law under the circumstances.[223]

Tyrannical judges have ruled otherwise, thus overruling the Constitution by judicial fiat.

The bottom line is this. The Founders believed you have a constitutional right to judge the law in a criminal case and *any judge who says otherwise* either hasn't studied our constitutional history or is a fool.

The purpose of republican government is to protect the individual's right to life, liberty and property. The Founders created a jury system to ensure that no one was convicted of a crime unless they violated the life, liberty or property of a fellow citizen. If you get a jury notice, don't grumble. Show up and exercise your rights and keep in mind that *no one* can tell you how to cast your vote in that jury room.

Now, just for the record, I'm not saying jurors should violate the law and lie to judges about their willingness to follow their instructions on the law. *What I'm saying is that judges should follow the law and should not lie to jurors!*

Take the silent oath:

> "If chosen to serve on a grand or petit jury, I will not indict or convict a defendant for any alleged crime when the alleged acts are peaceful and honest and with consenting adults. I understand that this is my right under the Sixth Amendment of the Constitution and I will not be bullied in the jury room to do otherwise."

6. Promote free market economics.

I have already explained how progressivism ignores and violates the laws of economics. A proper understanding of economics would make people immune to the progressive fallacy. Because there was no short overall summary of free market economics written in plain language, I wrote one a few years ago entitled "Economics in Five

---

[223] J. Ostrowski, "The Rise and Fall of Jury Nullification," 15 *Journal of Libertarian Studies* 89 (Spring 2001).

Lessons." It is posted at LibertyMovement.org. Please read the pamphlet and follow the links for a detailed study of economics especially at Mises.org. Then, send the link around to your contacts and print out copies and pass them around.

7. *Ostracize politicians.*

Politicians who refuse to change their ways even though there is overwhelming evidence they are destroying the country and imposing great harm on their own constituents and communities—should not be welcome in polite society. They should be ostracized and shunned. Instead, they are often treated like celebrities. This has to stop. Start treating them like the self-serving egomaniacs that they are.

Imagine a politician walking into the local diner. The owner comes up and says, "Joe, I don't know how to break this to you, but my customers don't want you in here. You will have to leave."

Wouldn't it be nice to see signs and bumper stickers pop up across America that say: **"Politician-Free Zone"**?

Don't be a sap and always fight your opponents with *their* weapons of choice and at the time and place of *their* choosing. Make these degenerate creeps fight on your own terms and on your own battlefield.

Surprise them! Revenge is a dish best served cold!

8. *Minimize your contacts with government.*

If you want smaller government, start acting like you mean it. Don't run off to this or that government agency whenever you have a problem. Start being self-reliant. Seek out private sector solutions to your problems. Look for problems in your neighborhood that you can solve without incurring the wrath of the state. Get your family, friends and neighbors involved, make it into a fun event and a teaching moment about the failure of government to solve problems. Here are some examples. (Follow LibertyMovement.org for more ideas.)

1. Cleaning up debris, litter, garbage and overgrown weeds in your neighborhood.

2. Liberate the sidewalks in your area by trimming trees that interfere with joggers, walkers, and young bikers.
3. Try to persuade families to pull out of the government schools.
4. Help *one person* get off the dole and ask them to pass the favor along to one other person and so on.
5. Encourage a private security firm such as Threat Management Center to begin serving your neighborhood. They have done wonders in Detroit.[224]

Whenever possible, avoid contacts with the government, especially the federal, state and county governments. Here are some examples.

- A few years ago, the City of Buffalo started busing Catholic school students. My wife and I refuse to use the service. It's not the government's job to get my kids to school. You can keep your slow, smelly, noisy and profanity-laced buses.

- The courts are clogged with petty criminal and civil matters. If you have a dispute with someone, don't use the police and courts as a free payback service. Try to resolve your problems in another way. Use private mediators or arbitrators to resolve minor civil disputes or just offer to buy the other fellow a cup of coffee.

- Don't buy lottery tickets. You are just giving the politicians more money to build their machines. You want to gamble? Buy stocks.

- When you give charitable donations, reward organizations that refuse to take government money.

---

[224] W. Grigg, "Call the Anti-Police: Ending the State's "Security" Monopoly," *LewRockell.com* (Sept. 17, 2014); see also Karen De Coster's blog, detroitrusttoriches.blogspot.com.

Granted, we are often forced to deal with the government. I am not asking you to be a hermit. All I am saying is, *when you have an option, avoid the government.* If you are going to talk about liberty, start living it!

9. Discourage people from working for the federal government.

The federal government of the United States is the greatest threat to liberty the American nation has ever faced. It is racing rapidly along the way toward a militaristic and totalitarian police state that will eventually control by brute force every significant choice we make or action we take.

As I explained in great detail in my first three books, *politics,* meaning elections and lobbying of various forms, has not enabled us to roll back the state. In fact, while the Liberty Movement has grown, so has the State and even more rapidly. I have urged the Movement to move most of its focus away from politics and toward direct citizen action, meaning *things that individuals can do today to directly move us towards liberty.* This has not yet happened though there is momentum on the homeschooling front.

Some in the Movement believe that any and all strategies and tactics are valuable and frown on anyone criticizing particular ones. How does it help the movement to waste huge amounts of resources including time, money, energy, historical opportunity, good will, and credibility on failed strategies and tactics that do not work? I can assure you that our enemies are ecstatic when our movement adopts failed strategies and tactics. For example, the political class loves it when we hold rallies because they know that 99% of these are a waste of time and not a threat to them in any sense; that they provide a relief valve for frustration that might otherwise be directed in more productive ways and that, by wasting the time, energy and money of activists, they ultimately cause burnout and despair leading to apathy and withdrawal from the Movement.

In short, *you are hurting the Movement* and helping our enemies when you adopt failed strategies and tactics, or fail to even consider the wisdom of them. Yet, these failed approaches persist. There are many reasons for this including inertia, "brainwashing" in government schools and lack of focus on the principles of strategy and tactics.

186

However, one overlooked reason why people adopt failed approaches can be explained by the subjective theory of value. Very often, failed approaches are more fun. They are more entertaining! Rallies are fun. Running for office can be exciting. Presidential elections can be thrilling. There's nothing intrinsically wrong with having fun, however, I contend that many activists prefer having fun to actually accomplishing anything. It's a huge problem for the movement and it's a huge problem for our country whose last, best hope is the Liberty Movement. If we don't get our acts together, who will? No one!

In that spirit, I am proposing a new tactic that can be considered a form of direct action as it involves neither elections nor lobbying in the standard sense. It's a simple concept but one which requires more work than fun and thus its ultimate success will be based on the movement's will to win. We know the movement likes to party. Do we want to win?

It is a principle of strategy in war, politics or sports to deprive your opponent of critical resources. For example, in basketball, we play aggressive offense to draw fouls to disqualify key players on the opposing team. In *Direct Citizen Action*, I proposed boycotting companies that are heavy political donors to discourage them from donating and therefore to starve the beast. I also favor voting with your feet along the lines proposed by the Free State Project but extending the principle to the county and municipal level. You can vote with your feet to lower your taxes and also to starve the beast of revenue.

Other than money, there is yet another resource critical to big government that needs to be addressed: labor. *Big government needs labor.* Everything government does is done by people. As government expands, it needs more and more employees. Obamacare required the hiring of 16,000 new IRS employees. Also, new workers must be hired to replace employees who retire, resign, die or become ill. There is a huge opportunity here for direct action.

First do no harm. *Under no circumstances should a libertarian work for the federal government.* That might seem obvious but I am certain there are such people. If you know one, ask them to consider resigning in protest over the rising tide of progressive totalitarianism if I may repeat myself.

Second, discourage your children from working for a murderous, corporatist, counterfeiting kleptocracy. If your children need you to sign papers to allow them to enlist in the Progressive State of America's imperialist standing army, *refuse*.

Third, discourage young people and people of any age from working for the kleptocracy. A series of arguments may be effective here.

Appeal to their own self-interest. Tell them they will be working in a bureaucracy where their own hard work and talent will *not* be rewarded. Their supervisor will be allowed to treat them arbitrarily and capriciously without any real fear of being penalized. They are shortchanging themselves by placing a severe limit on how far they can rise and how far their abilities can take them.

There are about 2.7 million civilian federal employees and another 1.4 million in the military. That's a total of 4.1 million people or about 1.3 percent of the population. According to the GAO, 30 percent of federal civilian workers could retire in the next three years.[225]

If you have older federal employees in your family or circle of friends, urge them to retire. They are certainly not going to be hurting on a federal pension yet they can still help the cause by leaving. About 100,000 people leave the federal government each year and about 100,000 sign up to replace them. In recent years, more people have left than joined, a good trend.

I think where progress can best be made, however, is with young people thinking about joining the Feds. It is much harder to get someone to resign or retire than to discourage a younger person from joining in the first place. That's where most of the effort should be expended.

Not all federal departments are equally critical to maintaining the progressive state. First, follow the money to the IRS. Without IRS workers harassing working Americans, the progressive state would lack the funds needed to maintain its control over us. We need to follow Thoreau's brilliant advice—long overlooked—in his great essay "Resistance to Civil Government":

---

[225] Source: money.cnn.com/2013/06/13/news/federal-workers-retire.

"If the tax-gatherer, or any other public officer, asks me, as one has done, 'But what shall I do?' my answer is, 'If you really wish to do anything, resign your office.' When the subject has refused allegiance, and the officer has resigned from office, then the revolution is accomplished."

Next, starve the federal law enforcement agencies that primarily target folks in the peaceful possession of private property (guns and drugs)—the DEA, FDA, ATF, etc. Finally, the third category of particularly odious departments are the spy agencies, FBI, CIA, and Homeland Security. We could do with a lot less poking and prodding of our bodies at airports, without the massive burglary of our private records, and without the assassination of foreign leaders and the instigation of foreign wars. If their entire history is any judge, the FBI will be unleashed on Liberty Movement activists in the coming years. The fewer agents "just following orders" the better.[226]

Henceforth, we need to make it *socially unacceptable to work for these government agencies* whose primary mission on a daily basis is to violate the very same natural rights the federal government was allegedly created to protect. See the Declaration of Independence.

10. Form your own leadership cell for liberty.

In forty years, the Liberty Movement has failed to create a national organization that would effectively organize the grassroots to challenge the Progressive State of America. It has been pointed out many times that the Liberty Movement is loaded with rugged individualists who don't like to be organized. That fact suggests an approach: leaderless resistance. *Let every Liberty Movement activist be his own organization.* Organize your family first, then your block, then your neighborhood.

If the French Revolutionaries taught us anything it is this: *the left is ruthless.* Their grandchildren the Bolsheviks reinforced the lesson. American progressives invented the nuclear bomb and used it. They

---

[226] J. Ostrowski, "History of the FBI," *Mises Daily* (Aug. 15, 2001).

bombed German and Japanese civilians. They put Japanese-Americans into concentration camps. *They have a 100-year history of harassing, intimidating, jailing and shooting political dissidents.*[227] If one person or a few persons lead a movement to topple them from power, they *will* retaliate and attempt to destroy them. That being the case, the leaderless resistance model is essential to our survival. Let *each of us* be Spartacus.

* * * * *

In the race between social power and state power, the smart money has always been on state power because of its awesome tangible assets: guns, troops, money, etc. Appearances can be deceiving, however. *The parasitical state is intrinsically weak* and must derive all of its resources from society by coercive means. Its ruling class is always small relative to society and is always in danger of losing its power which is why it depends upon on continuous propaganda and brainwashing to cover up its evil and destructive nature.

Politicians and government employees are themselves products of society. Like most persons, they seek social and community acceptance and approval and thus are extremely vulnerable to social power. A politician or federal employee who is a master of the universe one day can have his world shattered by social ostracism the next. Using the means described in this chapter, social power *can* defeat state power and without ever aping the violent tactics of its adversary.

* * * * *

These are effective strategies and tactics but we also need a bold gambit to dramatize our plight. We need a way to make it clear that *change is needed immediately!* There is, I am convinced, a lack of *urgency* in the Liberty Movement. For example, the main political strategy in the Movement currently is this: get Rand Paul elected President in 2016. He would take office in 2017! With a presumably hostile Congress, *maybe* by the end of his term, circa 2020!, he would have rolled back the *federal* budget by five percent. (State and local government will continue

---

[227] Started by the odious Woodrow Wilson.

to metastasize.) And even that scenario is unlikely given all the unlikely events that have to take place for it to happen, including his nomination (25% chance) and his election (40% chance). Thus, the bulk of Liberty Movement political resources will be *squandered* by a strategy whose initial premise, his actual election, has a ten percent chance of success. This is obviously a bad idea once properly defined and delineated.

Besides trying to elect a *conservative*[228] with neoconservative tendencies (Yikes!) to the presidency, there simply is no other plan for advancing liberty *right now*. To fill that void, I propose an idea that has been used in history but never by the Liberty Movement—the general strike.

On a certain day in the coming months, probably a Friday, we ask working people to strike, stay home from work. The exact date will be determined via social media by a consensus of activists. I don't expect enough people to do so to shut down the country but I think enough people will do so that a big impression will be made.

The main goal for the first event is simply to wake people up to the realization that we are sinking fast and cannot afford to wait for some ten-year plan for liberty. If there is no positive response by the power elite, we will hold another and much larger general strike two months later and so on until *demands* have been met. Each strike will be larger and will feature bolder and more creative tactics than the previous one. Eventually, the power elite will realize that either our demands will be met or American life simply will not continue as it did before.

The general strike will involve no violence or illegality. Such tactics betray a failure of the imagination and a failure to realize that *the State is inherently weak and is empowered by us*, by our acquiescence and tacit approval of its multifarious malefactions. This insight points the way to a peaceful and lawful protest movement. If there is to be any violence or illegality connected with these protests, the perpetrators will be our antagonists. The civil disobedience, the overthrowing of the Constitutional right to free speech and assembly, will be theirs, not ours.

---

[228] See Chapter 6.

How to Bury Progressivism and Restore American Liberty

A short list of common sense demands should be proposed, all of which should be designed to *immediately* lighten the load on working people and business owners in the country.

- **Bring the troops home** from the endless Asian land wars, cut military spending and use the savings to cut taxes.

  Savings: $100 billion

- **End the drug war**—use the savings to cut taxes!

  Savings: $50 billion

- **Sell off federal land** that has mineral wealth; use the savings to cut the federal debt; then use the savings on annual interest payments to cut taxes.

  Savings: $50 billion

- **Eliminate the gas tax.** It's killing working people and hurts businesses especially those that cater to travelers.

  Savings: $75 billion

- **Abolish the most useless federal agency, HUD**; give the current tenants deeds to their apartments; use the savings to cut taxes.

  Savings: $50 billion

- **Stop the portable tax collecting on the highways.** Issue tickets for reckless driving such as going 90 in a 30 or plowing through a red light at a crowded intersection near a school. Otherwise, stop picking our pockets to pad your oversized public pensions. Look into any traffic court in America and you will see hordes of sad-looking working people about to get fleeced by the same elected judges who supposedly represent their interests but who in fact are simply members of the greedy political class.

Savings: $10 billion

Total Annual Savings: $335 billion (that's real money).

The event should be fun and light-hearted, not grim. People don't like grim. They like fun. After some short rallies or meetings in localities, people should plan some fun activities for their rare day off.

Now, so many people are *not working* and sponging off the government that I thought that while the working class takes the day off, we would urge the *able-bodied*, non-working class *to actually work that day*, cleaning up trash and litter, whacking weeds and doing other volunteer work.

* * * * *

Finally, this book does not come close to exhausting all the possible strategies and tactics useful to creating a free society. Numerous other ideas from other sources will be listed at LibertyMovement.org as they come to our attention. We also need your own ideas. We can't do it alone. Too many times in our movement, organizations and campaigns have refused to accept outside feedback. LibertyMovement.org will be different. There will be a prominent portion of the website devoted to your own creative ideas for which you be will given full attribution if you wish. Please let us know about your own ideas, particularly ideas that have worked in your own communities. Remember what Emerson said: "in the work of every genius, we recognize our own rejected thoughts."

Conclusion

"The job of an orator is to discern events in their beginnings, foresee what is coming, and forewarn others."

~ Demosthenes

America is dying before our eyes from a misdiagnosis and misguided therapy: progressivism. Before progressivism, America was imperfect but far from sick. It didn't need the therapy of progressivism. The medicine is killing the patient! A society of free persons interacting with others only when, why and how they choose to do so is not sick but as healthy as one can hope for in this world.

Progressivism is not yet a fatal illness. If we stop taking the wrong medicine, we can recover and recover quickly. True liberty can quickly put us on the road to recovery, though the ill effects of progressivism will take some time to dissipate.

There is little time to dally, however. The trend lines are not good. They cannot continue but will ultimately slam into the brick wall of reality and explode. Take this two-part quiz:

1. List the major empires in history.
2. List all the ones that still exist.

The list shrinks from about fifteen to just one, the United States. Rome is gone. The Ottoman Empire is kaput. The British Empire is a memory as are the French and Spanish. The Soviet empire, which was thriving 25 years ago, has expired as did the Third Reich which at one time controlled most of Europe.

The United States is not immune to the forces of history and the laws of economics. It too can and will vanish, most likely in an exceedingly unpleasant manner, if it continues on its present path. It is easy to imagine scenarios where crises evolve into disasters, disasters into civil unrest and civil unrest into civil war. For example, hyperinflation to pay for explosive government spending could lead to calls for price controls; price controls will create shortages; shortages of essential goods could spark riots; riots could lead to a declaration of martial law. Martial law will not sit well with many Americans. There *will* be well-armed resistance. Inevitably, resistance will lead to skirmishes. When things advance to that point, no one can say that a civil war, perhaps a multiparty civil war, will not break out.

Civil war is often the bloodiest, most vicious kind of war. History shows that most wars are either sparked by racial, ethnic, or religious differences or those factors quickly come to play a part in how the wars are fought, by whom and against whom. In an increasingly multicultural nation, conflicts along those lines could easily occur. Worse yet, *there has never been a civil war within a state that is so well-armed with weapons of mass destruction.* Major defections from the military to join one side or another are foreseeable. Of course, they would bring their weapons with them. Who will get the nukes?

The above scenario is based on known facts, historical trends and common sense logical deductions based on how people tend to behave in such circumstances. If you think this nightmarish scenario cannot happen, you have failed to apprise yourself of the history of the human race, particularly the history of the bloody and progressive 20th century.

All of this can be avoided. The laws of nature, science and logic do not mandate that we should continue blithely down the road to slow-motion national suicide. Human beings have free will and *can* change their destinies. Americans of the past—*your* great-grandparents and even more distant relatives proved this by building from scratch the greatest nation that ever existed. Our task should be easier than theirs as we already have their example. It *can* be done because it has already been done.

Conclusion

I do believe in the old maxim, "whatever the mind can conceive and believe, it can achieve."[229] It has been proven time and again that "perseverance and spirit have down wonders in all ages."[230]

On the other hand, negativity, cynicism and pessimism become self-fulfilling prophecies. Those who seek bold change are decried as Don Quixoties by those who seek solace for their own callous indifference to the decline of their communities and the nation in the false notion that nothing can be done and only fools do not know that. The political class also delights in peddling cynicism and resignation, thus discouraging challenges to their power.

Big government rests on the pillars of negative emotions. Fear is chief among them, especially fear of failure. Envy is close behind. Envy and even greed may be strongly related to a lack of self-confidence. Lacking that confidence, many people tend to resent great achievers instead of trying to emulate them. Henry Veatch writes: a "lack of self-respect . . . is the sort of feeling that makes a man willing to sell his soul to the devil, and sometimes very cheaply too." That devil may be a "Hitler who promises such things as national glory and honor, to say nothing of food and employment, at the price of giving up one's critical intelligence and one's responsibility to think for oneself."[231]

Big government maestro FDR played off these fears and self-doubts and promised the Four Freedoms including freedom from "want" and "fear." FDR exploited people's lack of self-confidence and their *fear of failure*. This is how he helped turn a nation of free people into a nation ruled by free politicians.

Progressive big government is the word "No" writ large. No to freedom. No to reason. Ultimately, no to life itself. That's why its greatest accomplishment and proudest product is the nuclear bomb.

I coach youth basketball and concentrate on teaching kids how to shoot the ball. I have a three-part formula, form—aim—confidence (FAC). The most important element though is *confidence*. Why?

---

[229] Napoleon Hill.

[230] George Washington (1775).

[231] *Rational Man, A Modern Interpretation of Aristotelian Ethics*, Liberty Fund (2003), p. 65.

Conclusion

Because we have in our lives absorbed so much negative energy from those around us, especially the government, and I am convinced those negative thoughts seep deeply into our minds. They can determine the course of events. Deep down, the boys expect to miss that shot and, the body being the slave of the mind in such matters, more often than not, they do. The solution is to basically hypnotize yourself into thinking that every shot is going in. The results are truly amazing when the boys apply this approach.

So, if you are inclined to believe that all is hopeless, you are probably right because you have thereby taken yourself out of the fight. If, on the other hand, you believe that Liberty can prevail once more against its ancient foe, Power, then we can win *because you believe we can* and will join the fight with confidence that we will prevail.

The decision is yours.

Selected Bibliography

Bastiat, Frederick, "The Law," in *Selected Essays on Political Economy,* George B. de Huszar, ed. (Irvington-on-Hudson, N.Y.: Foundation for Economic Education, 1995).

Bovard, James, *Feeling Your Pain: The Explosion and Abuse of Government Power in the Clinton-Gore Year;* (New York: St. Martin's Press, 2000).

Courtoise, Stephane et al. *The Black Book of Communism* (Cambridge: Harvard University Press, 1999).

Creveld, Martin Van, *The Rife and Decline of the State* (New York: Cambridge University Press, 1999).

Denson, John (ed.) *Reassessing the Presidency): the Rise of the Executive State and the Decline of Freedom* (Auburn, AL: Mises Institute, 2001).

Denson, John V. (ed.) *The Costs of War* (New Brunswick, NJ: Transaction Publishers, 1997).

DiLorenzo, Thomas, *The Real Lincoln* (NY: Prima Publishing, 2002).

Ebeling, Richard M. and Hornberger, Jacob G., *The Failure of America's Foreign Wars* (Fairfax, VA: Future of Freedom Foundation, 1996).

Gordon, David, Ed. *Secession, State, and Liberty.* (New Brunswick, N.J.: Transaction Publishers, 1998).

Hazlitt, Henry, *Economics in One Lesson* (Fiftieth Anniversary Edition, San Francisco: Pox & Wilkes, 1996).

Higgs, Robert, *Crisis and Leviathan: Critical Episodes in the Growth of Government* (New York: Oxford University Press, 1987).

Holzer, Henry Mark, *Sweet Land of Liberty?* (Costa Mesa, CA: The Common Sense Press, Inc., 1983).

Selected Bibliography

Hoppe, Hans-Hermann, *Democracy: the God That Failed* (New Brunswick, NJ: Transaction Publishers, 2002).

Hoppe, Hans-Hermann, Ed., *The Myth of National Defense: Essays on the Theory and History of Security Production* (Mises Institute, 2003).

La Boetie, Etienne de. *The Politics of Obedience: The Discourse of Voluntary Servitude.* (New York: Free Life Editions, 1975).

Lepage, Henri, *Tomorrow, Capitalism: The Economics of Economic Freedom* (London: Open Court Publishing Company, 1978).

Locke, John, *The Second Treatise of Civil Government* (1690).

Mises, Ludwig van, *Human Action: The Scholar's Edition* (Auburn, AL: Mises Institute, 1998 [1949]).

_____ *Liberalism: A Socio-Economic Exposition* (1927), trans. Ralph Raico (Kansas City: Sheed Andrews and McMeel, 1978).

_____ *Socialism: An Economic and Sociological Analysis* (Liberty Classics: Indianapolis, 1981).

Nozick, Robert. *Anarchy, State, and Utopia.*

Oppenheimer, Franz, *The State: Its History and Development Viewed Sociologically* (New York: Vanguard Press, 1926).

Ostrowski, James, *Direct Citizen Action: How We Can Win the Second American Revolution without Firing a Shot* (Cazenovia Books: Buffalo, NY 2010).

_____ *Government Schools Are Bad for Your Kids: What You Need to Know* (Cazenovia Books: Buffalo, NY 2009).

_____ *Political Class Dismissed: Essays Against Politics* (Cazenovia Books: Buffalo, NY 2004).

Selected Bibliography

Paul, Ellen Frankel; Miller, Fred D.; Paul, Jeffrey, eds., *Natural Rights Individualism and Progressivism in American Political Philosophy* (Cambridge University Press, 2012).

Raimondo, Justin, *An Enemy of the State* (Prometheus Books: Amherst, N.Y., 2000)

Rand, Ayn, *Atlas Shrugged.*

_____ *The Fountainhead.*

Reisman, George. *Capitalism: A Treatise on Economics.*

Rockwell, Llewellyn H., *Speaking of Liberty* (Auburn, AL: Mises Institute, 2003)

Rothbard, Murray N., *America's Great Depression* (Auburn, AL: Mises Institute, 2000 [1963]).

____ *Austrian Perspective on the History of Economic Thought* (2 vols., London: Edward Elgar, 1995).

_____ *Conceived In Liberty* (4 vols.) (Auburn, AL: Mises Institute, 1999).

____ *For a New Liberty,* (Collier Books: New York, rev. ed. 1978).

____ *Man, Economy, and State* (Auburn, AL: Mises Institute, 1993, 1962).

____ *Power and Market: Government and the Economy* (Kansas City: Sheed Andrews and McMeel, 1970)

____ *The Ethics* of *Liberty* (Atlantic Highlands, N.J.: Humanities Press, 1982).

Selected Bibliography

_____ *What Has Government Done to Our Money?* (Auburn, AL: Mises Institute, 1990).

Rummel, R.]. *Death by Government.* New Brunswick, N.J.: Transaction Books, 1994.

Schoeck, Helmut, *Envy* (Indianapolis: Liberty Classics, 1981 (1948».

Spooner, Lysander, *No Treason: The Constitution of No Authority (1870).*

Szasz, Thomas, *Our Right to Drugs: The Case for a Free Market* (New York: Praeger, 1992).

Tannehill, Morris and Linda, *The Market for Liberty,* (New York: Laissez-Faire Books, Inc., 1984).

Trenchard, John, et al, *Cato's Letters.* Ed. By Ronald Hamowy.

Index

Adams, John, 106
African-Americans, 17
Alien and Sedition laws, 104
American System, 153
Americans with Disabilities Act, 124
Anderson, Martin, 114
Antifederalist No. 1, 131
Antitrust, 66, 83
Aquinas, Thomas, 175
Art subsidies, 88
ATF, 189
Augustine, St., 175
Bailyn, Bernard, 95
Barnett, Randy, 32, 33
Bastiat, Frederic, 52, 101, 102
Berg, Chris, 102
Black Friday, 11
Bolsheviks, 145, 149, 189
Bovard, James, 86
Brandeis, Louis, 114
Bright, John, 100
Britain, 178
British Empire, 195
Bush, George, 179
Callahan, Gene, 52
Carlson, Allan, 70
Cato Institute, iv, 79
Cato's Letters, 94, 95, 103
Churchill, Winston, 100, 163
CIA, 101, 189

civil rights, 17, 110, 118
Civil War, 2, 47, 48, 64, 68, 70, 105, 107, 129, 137, 138, 143, 144
Clarence, New York, 179
Clinton, Bill, 100, 124, 125
Cobden, Richard, 100, 103
coercion, 177
Communism, 178
Comprehensive Employment and Training Act (CETA), 27
Confederacy, 138, 154
conscription, 47, 61, 65, 113, 142, 143, 153, 155, 160
consent, 32, 33
conservatism, 119, 123, 124, 125, 126, 127, 131, 134
Constant, Benjamin, 31
Constitution, 32, 47, 104, 105, 106, 115, 129, 130, 131, 183
constitutionalism, 129, 130, 131, 133
Continental Army, 91
Coolidge, Calvin, 123
credit card debt, 11
crime, 176
Cromwell, 94
Cuomo, Mario, 152
daycare, 13, 14, 70
DEA, 189
Dean, Paula, 17

Index

Debs, Eugene V., **106, 160**

Declaration of Independence, **33, 94, 157, 189**

Democratic Party, **179**

Democrats, **179**

Demosthenes, **195**

Department of Education, **178**

Depression, the, **178**

Dewey, John, **48, 140**

Dewey, Thomas E., **123**

Diabetes, **12**

DiLorenzo, Thomas, **85, 152, 162**

direct citizen action, **182**

Direct Citizen Action, **v, 187, 214**

Discourses Concerning Government, **96**

Dole, Bob, **5**

drug overdoses, **13, 79**

drugs, **176, 177**

Duck Dynasty, **17**

Duranty, Walter, **148**

economics, **80, 127, 178**

Edison, Thomas, **54**

Egalitarianism, **41, 42, 43**

Eisenhower, Dwight D., **123, 139**

Emerson, **75, 99, 193**

eminent domain, **61, 65**

English Civil War, **93**

Envy, **42, 43, 197**

epistemological, **86**

epistemology, **49**

Espionage Act of 1917, **106**

FBI, **130, 189**

FDA, **79, 80, 189**

FDR, **178**

Federal Reserve, **2, 7, 9, 38, 68, 83, 123, 139, 160, 179**

Feffer, Andrew, **1**

First Amendment, **42, 104, 108, 109**

Ford, Henry, **54**

Free State Project, **181, 187**

Freedom of travel., **115**

French Revolution, **41, 43**

French Revolution., **41**

Fugitive Slave law, **153**

G. I. Bill, **129**

Galloway, Lowell, **69**

gas tax, **192**

gay rights, **114**

general strike, **191**

global empire, **179**

global military empire, **179**

Goldwater, Barry, **123**

government schools, **3, 13, 16, 26, 27, 33, 37, 38, 54, 55, 65, 66, 68, 73, 74, 85, 91, 98, 148, 174, 176, 177, 178, 179, 180, 186**

Government schools, **175, 176, 177, 180**

Government Schools Are Bad for Your Kids, **iv, 46, 65, 71, 74, 175, 214**

Great Depression, **68, 139, 162**

Great Society, **2, 18, 127, 129, 139**

Greene, J. P., **176**

Gulf War, **127, 142**

habeas corpus, **103, 105, 125, 154**

Hamilton, Alexander, **14, 105, 106**

Harding, Warren, **123, 160, 161**

Harper, F. A., **80**

Harrison Act of 1914, **160**

Index

Hayek, Friedrich, 125, 126, 165, 168

Hazlitt, Henry, 52, 80

hedonism, 177

Heritage Foundation, 10

Higgs, Robert, 52

Hitler, 24, 31, 49, 100, 151, 163, 197

Hodgskin, Thomas, 113, 114

Holmes, Oliver Wendell, 1, 64, 106, 107, 108, 109, 110, 114

Holmes., Oliver Wendell, 1, 106

Homeland Security, 189

Hoover, Herbert, 68, 123

Hoppe, Hans-Hermann, 12, 52, 57, 62, 63, 65, 145, 146

House of Representatives, 37

HUD, 192

Hülsmann, Guido, ii, 9

human capital, 11, 12, 13, 65, 66

hyperinflation, 8, 42, 196

incarceration, 16

income tax, 2, 38, 47, 123, 158, 159, 160

Industrial Revolution, 98, 99

inflation, 2, 9, 12, 27, 48, 61, 65, 70, 72, 124, 142

IRS, 162, 187, 188

James, William, 48

Jefferson, Thomas, i, 94, 100, 104, 105, 106, 107, 116

Jesus, 45, 174, 175

Jim Crow, 17

Job training, 27, 66, 87

Job Training Partnership Act of 1982, 27

Jobs, Steve, 54

Johnson, Chalmers, 179

Johnson, Lyndon, 100, 124, 139, 157, 163, 164, 165

judges, 182, 183

juries, 182

jury nullification, 182

Kennedy, John F., 139

knockout game, 17

Landon, Alf, 123

leaderless resistance, 189, 190

Lee, Spike, 17

Lenin, 179

Leno, Jay, 14

Levellers, 93, 94

LewRockwell.com, 33, 64, 86, 117

liberal, 179

liberalism, 18, 21, 22, 23, 29, 30, 42, 44, 49, 51, 57, 71, 91, 92, 93, 97, 98, 99, 100, 108, 117, 118, 119, 120, 121, 123, 134, 146, 165, 170

Liberalism, v, 21, 22, 23, 42, 91, 92, 93, 98, 111, 119

libertarian, iv, 1, 38, 76, 91, 99, 114, 168, 169, 183

Libertarian Party, iv, 38, 169

Liberty Movement, iii, iv, v, 3, 6, 114, 118, 134, 168, 169, 170, 172, 182, 186, 187, 189, 190, 191

LibertyMovement.org, i, 171, 172, 174, 184, 193

Lilburne, John, 93

Lincoln, Abraham, 41, 46, 47, 48, 151, 152

Lochner v. New York, 110

Locke, John, 94, 95, 102, 113, 116

lottery tickets, 185

Index

Madison, James, 104
majority rule, 179
Manhattan Institute, 176
Marx, 24, 31, 49, 149
Mason, George, 91, 104, 180
McAdam, Jane, 115
McKinley, William, 157
McPherson, James, 47
Medicaid, 2, 38, 70, 77, 78, 164
Medicare, 2, 38, 77, 124, 164
Mencken, H. L., 100, 108, 109, 111
minimum wage, 2, 38, 76, 125
Mises, Ludwig von, 9, 23, 41, 52, 78, 92, 139, 178
Molinari, Gustave de, 100
multiculturalism, 118
natural rights, 31, 33, 41, 42, 43, 44, 49, 94, 96, 102, 104, 106, 107, 109, 110, 114, 115, 120, 153, 189
Nazi Germany, 120
New Deal, 2, 18, 48, 68, 69, 71, 139, 162, 163, 178
New York State United Teachers, 179
Nietzsche, 112
Ninth Amendment, 115
Nixon, Richard, 100, 114, 123, 162
Nock, Albert Jay, 18, 100, 102
Nozick, Robert, iii, 43, 112
NSA, 15, 16
Obama, 179
Obama, Barack, 15, 87, 157
Obamacare, 78, 125, 187
Obesity, 11, 13
Occupational Licensure, 66

Orwell, 145
Orwell, George, 21
Ottoman Empire, 58, 195
Overton, Richard, 93
Paterson, Isabel, 178
Patriots, 182
Patterson, Isabel, 151
Paul, Rand, 190
Paul, Ron, i, iv, 38, 115, 169, 170, 179
Peirce, Charles, 48
Pol Pot, 120
politicians, 32, 184, 185
Politicians, 184
Pope John Paul II, 78
Pork Lawsuit, 129, 131
Postmillennial Pietism, 45
Powell, Jim, 86, 102, 158
pragmatism, 41, 48, 49, 62, 87
Progressive Era, 2, 4, 41, 73, 137, 157, 168
Progressive Movement, 46
Progressive State of America, 5, 13, 64, 175, 188, 189
propaganda, 178
property taxes, 181
Prussia, 176
psychotropic drugs, 177
Race relations, 17
Raico, Ralph, 21, 22, 93, 97, 99, 140, 141
Raimondo, Justin, 15
Rand, Ayn, iii, 63, 119
Reagan, Ronald, 123, 124, 169
redistribution, 56, 57
regulation, 2, 57, 79, 83
Regulation, 2, 83, 84
regulations, 180, 181

Index

religion, 177
republic, 178, 179
republican government, 183
Republican Revolution of 1994, 169
Robert "Brutus" Yates, 131
Robertson, Phil, 17
Rockefeller, John D., 158
Rockwell, Lew, 33
Rome, 46, 195
Romney, Mitt, 170
Roosevelt, Franklin D., 67, 68, 70, 88, 124, 129, 139, 159, 161, 162, 163, 197
Roosevelt, Theodore, 41, 46, 47, 137, 157
Rothbard, Murray, iii, iv, 1, 9, 18, 19, 22, 24, 29, 31, 41, 43, 45, 46, 52, 55, 84, 92, 93, 94, 95, 100, 123, 139, 143, 151, 157
Rousseau, 41, 43
Ruby Ridge, 121
Rudyard Kipling, Rudyard, iv, 157
Ruger, William P., 180
Rummel, R. J., 114
Say, J. B., 97
Second Amendment, 42
Selective Service Act of 1917, 30, 114
Sidney, Algernon, 94, 96
Simpson, O. J., 17
Sixth Amendment, 183
slavery, 17, 45, 98, 101, 102, 114, 120, 137, 153, 156
Smith, George, 96, 99, 113
Smoot Hawley Tariff, 68
Social contract, 31
Social security, 67, 68

Social Security, 2, 3, 27, 28, 38, 66, 69, 70, 124, 129
Socialized medicine, 66, 76
Sorens, Jason, 180, 181
Soviet Communism, 53
Spanish-American War, 5
Spencer, Herbert, 100, 110, 115
Spooner, Lysander, 100
Stalin, 31, 100, 148, 161, 163, 178
Stalinist Russia, 120
student loans, 8, 75, 129
Sumner, William Graham, 100
Sweden, 70
Tax Foundation, 181
taxes, 32, 181
Tea Party movement, 169
Third Reich, 196
Thomas More, Saint, 147
Thoreau, 188
Tocqueville, Alexis de, 68, 105
Trenchard and Gordon, 94, 95, 103, 104
Truman, Harry, 100
Twain, Mark, 158, 159, 161
Unemployment insurance, 10
unions, 2, 80, 81, 163, 179
utopia, 24, 26, 147, 148, 176
utopianism, 27, 29, 30, 46, 88, 147, 148
Veatch, Henry, 197
Vedder, Richard, 69
Vietnam, 127, 139, 142, 144, 164
violence, 32
Virginia Declaration of Rights, 104
von Kuehnelt-Leddihn, Eric, 49
Voting, 32

Index

Waco, **121**

Walwyn, William, **93**

War, **179**

War of 1812, **143**

war on drugs, **17, 38, 73, 101, 124, 126, 148, 160**

war on poverty, **73, 101, 127, 128, 164**

Washington, **181**

Washington, George, **54, 197**

weapons, **184**

welfare, **2, 9, 16, 17, 27, 30, 38, 44, 70, 72, 73, 101, 118, 123, 125, 127, 139, 148, 155, 158, 174, 175, 179**

Wenzel, Robert, **6**

Whig Party (British), **91**

Willkie, Wendell, **123**

Wilson, Woodrow, **23, 100, 106, 114, 124, 142, 144, 148, 157, 159, 160, 161, 163, 190**

Workforce Investment Act of 1998, **27**

World War I, **6, 18, 30, 31, 68, 86, 106, 109, 114, 129, 140, 141, 142, 144, 145, 160, 163**

World War II, **178**

About the Author

James Ostrowski is a trial and appellate lawyer and author from Buffalo, New York. He graduated from St. Joseph's Collegiate Institute in 1975 and obtained a degree in philosophy from the State University of New York at Buffalo in 1980. He graduated from Brooklyn Law School in 1983. In law school, he was writing assistant to Dean David G. Trager, later a federal judge in the Eastern District of New York. He was a member of the Moot Court Honor Society and the International Law Moot Court Team.

He served as vice-chairman of the law reform committee of the New York County Lawyers Association (1986-88) and wrote two widely quoted reports critical of the law enforcement approach to the drug problem. He was chair of the human rights committee, Erie County Bar Association (1997-1999). He has written a number of scholarly articles on the law on subjects ranging from drug policy to the commerce clause of the constitution.

His articles have appeared in the Wall Street Journal, Buffalo News, Cleveland Plain Dealer and Legislative Gazette. His policy studies have been published by the Hoover Institution, the Ludwig von Mises Institute, and the Cato Institute in Washington, D.C. His articles have been used as course materials at numerous colleges including Brown, Rutgers and Stanford.

He is the author of *Political Class Dismissed (2004)*, *Government Schools Are Bad for Your Kids (2009)* and *Direct Citizen Action (2010)*. Presently, he is an adjunct scholar at the Ludwig von Mises Institute and a columnist for LewRockwell.com.

He and his wife Amy live in North Buffalo with their two children, Anna and Will. He is a long-time youth baseball and basketball coach.

Made in the USA
San Bernardino, CA
23 May 2016